'Significant and effective leadership flows from character, and character growth requires the nourishing of our souls. Karl has carefully and clearly explored four ways in which our leadership can be deeply rooted in this approach. This is a book that I wish had been read by every leader before they stepped up to the task. It could not be more relevant to our time.'

PETE WYNTER
DIRECTOR, LEADERSHIP COLLEGE LONDON

'Karl possesses an innate and extensive understanding of those of us in leadership roles, and the obstacles that can hinder our effectiveness. Karl's deep commitment to providing essential catalysts for more impactful leadership makes this book a repeat read; and with each read, it's clear the author walks the talk in his leadership of leaders.'

KIMBERLY INSKEEP
EXECUTIVE CHAIRMAN, CABI HOLDINGS

'Karl is a trusted voice in my life and this book is full of his wisdom. Read it and apply it – you will be a better leader and a better person.'

FREDDIE FREEMAN
LA DODGERS

'Karl works with so many successful business leaders and team builders and has become a successful coach in today's complicated business environment. This book is a valuable read.'

COACH JOE GIBBS
OWNER AND FOUNDER, JOE GIBBS RACING

'Karl is a gift and his guiding words have become recurring strength in my life. He has a way of communicating that is uniquely inspirational and incredibly necessary in today's complicated world. I am grateful for him; I am sure you will be, too.'

LINDA YACCARINO
CEO OF X

'This wonderful book burns with wisdom and warmth because its author, Karl Martin, combines one of the sharpest minds with one of the softest hearts of anyone I know. His hard-won insights have been distilled and field-tested again and again in diverse contexts, over many years. In a world awash with trendy techniques to help people become better leaders, this is a message to help leaders become better people. Which is really all that matters in the end.'

PETE GREIG
FOUNDER, 24-7 PRAYER INTERNATIONAL

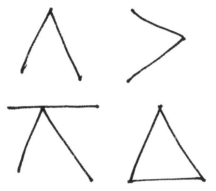

KARL MARTIN

with Stephanie Heald

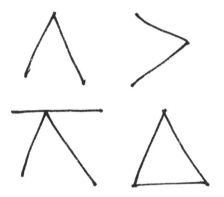

THE CAVE, THE ROAD, THE TABLE AND THE FIRE

LEADING FROM A DEEPER PLACE

Kilfinan
Press

Published in 2023 by
Kilfinan Press, Edinburgh, Scotland.

Reprinted 2024

www.kilfinanpress.com

books@kilfinanpress.com

© Karl Martin 2023

Illustrations © Karl Martin 2023

Karl Martin has asserted his right under the Copyright, Designs and Patents Act 1988 to be
identified as the author of this work.

Kilfinan Press is an imprint of Muddy Pearl Ltd.

British Library Cataloguing in Publication Data.

A catalogue record for this book is available from the British Library

ISBN 978-1-914553-25-7

Typeset in Minion by Revo Creative Ltd, Lancaster

Printed in Great Britain by Bell & Bain Ltd, Glasgow

CONTENTS

FOREWORD

'Jack, I want you to meet a guy I know, he's different. I think he possesses what you are looking for.'

I first met Karl in extraordinary circumstances. I had been looking for an executive coach for almost five years and had never found the right fit. I had just about given up the search – resigned to gathering whatever wisdom I could from books, courses and occasional interactions – when the Covid-19 virus hit the planet. It was then that a mutual friend introduced us. While I never want a global pandemic to ever devastate us again, I am extremely grateful that it led me to the coach I knew I needed and couldn't find.

BOOM … one Zoom call and thirty minutes later, I was convinced Karl and his coaching was exactly what I had been lacking. Quickly, we decided to pursue a connection that turned into a contract and has become a real partnership. From day one, my interactions with him, his understated wisdom and direct challenge have made me a stronger, more confident, relational leader. As you engage with his writing in this book, my hope is that it will do the same for you.

Quite early on in our engagement, it became clear to me that Karl's style and system was going to have a powerful impact, not only on my personal leadership journey but also for my team, my organization and even my family. At Toyota, Karl has helped me build 'The Super Six' which is my entire Toyota/Lexus leadership team. Karl has become a sought-after resource for our entire company, and I can't stop recommending him and his consultancy to other executives. Perhaps most importantly, Karl has become my friend; a great friend and a golf partner as well as a thought partner. In the book you are about to read, Karl talks about 'influences' and describes a city, asking you to decide who gets access to you and how. He and his wife Niki have gained access to my life – my wife, my kids, my friends – and we are all richer for it. I'm beginning to think that that's the superpower at work here – clients become friends; colleagues become friends; even readers become friends. It feels a little counterintuitive even to type this, but perhaps that's what happens when, as Karl puts it, 'you lead from your soul' and encourage others to do so too.

I'm not sure exactly how to describe his leadership style and system to you and you will gather more as you read, but let me have a go.

As you read *The Cave, the Road, the Table and the Fire*, you will encounter not just an author who could become your friend but an incisive and provocative executive coach. When I started working with Karl I realized, as our introducer had intimated, that he was different. When you meet him, in person or in the stories written here, you will meet a strange amalgam of personal mentor, intellectual provocateur and spiritual guide. He's wholehearted, bold and a relationally brilliant leader; his business bleeds this stuff and so does the book. Reading it, I can quite literally hear his voice in my head. It took me back to conversations we had and lessons that I'd actioned. It is not often that a book sounds like the one who wrote it ... this one does. It's even less common for the words on a page to be as impactful as a coach in a room, but I think the words in this book just might be.

What I know you will find in the pages that follow is a philosophy and practice that is deeply personal and truly bespoke. Karl's approach is not the normal, 'here are my ten steps to success' or 'this is my program; just follow it'. Instead, his system is all about personal responsibility, empathic wisdom, and radical contextualizing. It starts where you are and moves you to where you want to be, where you need to be, for you to lead in the room and in the way you were made to lead.

In some ways, I guess this book is like so many others: full of useful models, concepts and tools that will grow your skillset. Yet, in other ways, it is like the author: different. I believe what it's really trying to do is to invite you into a True, Brave, Kind and Curious leadership revolution; one designed to reframe the very nature of leadership and promising to bring about the kind of change that is desperately needed in our chaotic culture. If you engage with it, as I have engaged with Karl, I believe it could have the same effect on you as he has had on me.

And it needs to!

Leadership, as Karl puts it, is the greatest of human gifts. I have always thought so and built my career trying to grow mine and the leadership of those around me. As Karl points out later in this book, I have always carried a belief that people are our greatest asset. In business, and in life, your people are more important than your profit. In truth, it is the only way you get one. I guess that the virtues taught here would, traditionally, be regarded as 'soft skills'. However, I have come to regard them as 'vital skills'. Sadly, these vital skills are rarely mastered, often missing and badly needed in corporate America at this time.

As you read and study, you will discover a 'fixing of the soul' that is deeper than a solving of a problem. You will find that the principles and patterns in this book are ancient and yet deeply relevant; they are at times spiritual (his personal faith clearly underpins his thinking), but they are always practical – above all, they work!

This really works!

Since meeting with Karl and working with him, I have been promoted to EVP of Toyota North America and President of Toyota USA. My direct reports are benefiting hugely from the insights in this book and have become more aligned and focused as a result. Even my family has been encouraged (my golf – not so much) but THAT is a whole different story.

In the chapters outlining 'the Table' Karl unpacks what was perhaps the most impactful conversations that he and I have had around the nature of trust: how you grow it and how you measure it. *Did my team trust one another? Could they? Did they trust me?* I had always believed that the amount of trust in a team or company was the key factor in determining the performance of the group, but the discipline of unpacking and applying that conversation and coaching session has become the central component to my Toyota team's subsequent development. You will find it laid out in this book as an equation:

$$Trust = \frac{Credible + Dependable + Relatable}{Selfish}$$

As I studied this with him and then read it again here, what I realized is that Karl lives this stuff and that this book is full of it. Credible; Dependable; Relatable. He wants you to KNOW you and it allows you to know him.

Friends, if you read this book carefully, apply the learning and adopt the patterns, you will lead better. How much better, I truly believe is on you. Trust the book, the author and the process.

Let me end by offering a public health warning:

This book will change you, IF you let it! Karl is a disruptor! Concepts will challenge you, stories will move you and models will guide you, IF you let it! Your work and your personal life will be expanded and enhanced, IF you let it!

Karl makes the point, towards the end of the book, that some of us are just not teachable, just not curious enough to grow, just not ready to 'let it'.

Folks, I am encouraging you to go for it! Go hard after the lessons articulated here and allow yourself to be your best you.

As he says, 'you are the project'. In my experience that's always the case. Please take this on; take it to mean it's on you before it is on anyone else. You will grow your leadership if you truly embrace this book. SO? Buckle up, strap yourself in, let's read and then let's lead … better.

Jack Hollis
EVP, TOYOTA NORTH AMERICA AND PRESIDENT, TOYOTA USA.
Texas, October 2023

ACKNOWLEDGEMENTS

To my team, Arable – by name and nature.

To S, my publisher and the best editor a writer could have. For wisdom, skill and collaboration.

To J & K and J & J, supporters and challengers. Friends who have become family.

To L, K, A, S and E. Your leadership makes me proud, your potential makes me hopeful.

And to N, my '*cymbrogi*', my soulmate. Without whom none of this works.

Thank you, thank you.

THE PROJECT

'*You are the project.*'

He almost whispered, but I heard it as a roar.

'*The project is not the project; you are the project. The product is not the project, the strategy is not the project, the vision is not even the project. YOU ARE.*'

He was a man I'd admired from afar – revered, an expert, possibly the best in his field. And that was his best opening?

I sat confused, offended, alone amid a few hundred other young leaders, all ambitious and keen to learn and master any new approach to the art of influencing people. And this just messed with my head. It directly challenged my assumptions, my disposition, and exposed my natural inclination to short-cut my way to success with soundbites, new ideas and a few smart tactics.

That moment effectively ruined me for any other perspective on leadership.

I am the project.

What he was pointing out was that leadership doesn't exist without a leader; it's a person before it's ever a concept or a system. If you strip away all the leadership noise – the podcasts streamed, the books read or written, the strategies adopted – you're left with a leader.

This is about *that*.

This is about unearthing who you really are; unlocking the very deepest part of you; this is about unveiling what I like to call soul. (I'll get down to explaining this more in the coming chapters.)

The project *is* you.

SO . . .
Draw a circle on the ground.
Don't stop reading because it just got practical. Do it – draw!

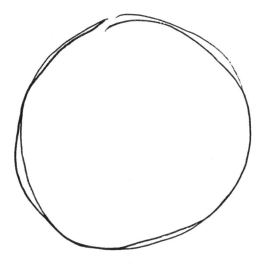

If you happen to be on a beach, do it in the sand. If you are on your patio, do it with a chalk stone. If, as is likely, you are neither, draw your circle with your finger – just imagine the circle on the floor in front of you. Now, step inside it. And own everything within the circle.

What I'm asking is, before you address anything outside the boundary, will you take responsibility for all that is inside of it? Will you address all that is in yourself? All dreams, all fears, all possibilities, all limitations, all wounds, all merits, all gifts.

All.

The tale of the circle maker[1] has different central characters, depending on which tradition you're storied in. It might be a Rabbi called Honi, who prayed for rain, or a preacher called Gipsy, who asked for favour. It might be a real story or made up. But the point is the same: It's on you. You are responsible; you are your first responsibility.

It's the best starting point for all that follows. Get in the circle. Put yourself in the story. You are the project. And stay there. Staying is an act of focused ownership.

I don't care whether you sit, so as to say, *'I will not move from here. This is the project.'* Or whether you stand, posturing, *'It's on me. I am the project.'* Or whether you kneel, acknowledging, *'This is a moment. I submit myself as the project.'* What we're aiming at is a humble ownership that comes from a much deeper place. The transformation that could flow *from* you must grow *in* you.

The project is leading yourself, so you can lead others. And then groups of others, who lead others. It requires a digging, it will be challenging in every good way and then worth every effort you make. This is, after all, about leadership. The greatest skill you could ever develop. The ability to influence, inspire and transform; to grow people, manage systems and organize structures.

For some reading this, it will sound like an overstatement, but my experience tells me leadership is all. It's everything. Everything you need to grow something, inspire someone, change someplace. Show me a great team, and I'll show you great leadership. Whether that team is a national government, a business, a charity, a sports franchise or a family – the success or failure of that team is largely dependent on the quality of its leadership. The quality of its leader. Show me chaos, infighting, underperformance, a victim or blame culture, and I will show you a failure of leadership. Of a leader.

1 Mark Batterson, *The Circle Maker: Praying Circles Around Your Biggest Dreams and Greatest Fears* (Zondervan, 2016), pp22–25.

Criminally, this greatest skill is usually learned as a catch-up measure or a reverse engineering exercise. Acquired accidentally or incidentally 'on the job', often only taught intentionally, far down the road, as gaps are revealed. The greatest human skill has been relegated to a 'nice to have'. Or a 'soft skill'. We teach technical skills as a logical expedience and neglect the most transformational of callings.

And so, we have a generation of leaders equipped to manage process, but not to lead people. Leadership has become positional – all about a title. It's become suffocatingly superficial – all about a product or a profit. It's barely functional, flimsy and broken.

But it could be so much more.

And it must be, because the stakes are high. We're talking about you fulfilling your life's potential. We're also talking about you leading others to do the same. But more broadly, you are reading this in a moment of leadership crisis where people are avoiding formal positions of influence, and when they fall into them, are ill-equipped to deliver health. Leadership itself is in crisis.

If you don't believe me, read the newspaper. Every day for a week. Allow me to summarize what you'll find: politicians with flimsy morals, populist agenda and a culture of massive polarization. Sports managers given payoffs and system-wide corruption. Financial leaders bullying and eroding trust in big business. Religious leaders abusing power and becoming increasingly compromised. Heads of state whose personal lives and ethical choices are undermining their ability to call anyone to a higher standard.

The role of leadership in the workplace, in the family, and in the community has eroded, and is even resented.

'You are the project' is the Truth that whispers and then screams, refusing to allow us to shake our heads, wring our hands, justify our position or blame someone else.

No! Stay in the circle and a different kind of leader might emerge.

INTRODUCTION

21 GRAMS (AND YOUR DOG MISSED OUT)

The weight of your soul is 21 grams.

That is, at least, according to Duncan MacDougall, a physician,[2] and Alejandro Iñárritu, the director of a film of the same title, *21 Grams*, starring Sean Penn.[3] In 1907, MacDougall attempted a spurious scientific experiment to measure the weight lost from a human being when the soul left the body. One of the six bodies experimented on lost ¾ of an ounce or 21.3 grams. So, he hypothesized, your soul exists! He later set up an experiment with dogs, discovering nothing was lost postmortem and concluding dogs did not have souls, while human beings did.

I'm pretty sure MacDougall's pseudo-science or Iñárritu's artistic point that your soul has mass you can weigh isn't true. And one can't avoid the controversy around how MacDougall happened to be present at the death of so many dogs! The desire to show soul as a foundational part of human life was a noble one, but to prove it by measuring its mass seems absurd. For something to be of vital influence in our lives, it does not need physical mass. The power of thought, feeling, emotion, culture and tradition all impact us in ways many of their material counterparts could only dream about.

Here's my own hypothesis. The core of you is soul. Deeper than personality, and much more than a body responding to a material world through the activity of five senses. That soul is reflective consciousness; it is, right now, informing mind, will and emotions. The immaterial you directing the material you.

2 Rachel Armstrong, Simone Ferracina, Rolf Hughes, *Liquid Life: On Non-Linear Materiality* (Punctum Books, 2019), p245.
3 Alejandro González Iñárritu, dir., *21 Grams* (Focus Features, 2003).

As such, the soul is not only the essence of who you are, it also carries the truth of who you might become. It is the noblest, bravest and most creative and collaborative part of us; as such, soul leadership changes relationships and circumstances for the better. It brings dreams to life, enriches communities, offers safety and hope. Soul leaders raise soul leaders.

But we don't teach about soul. Or advocate for it in the leadership conversation. Perhaps it is too religious in overtone or too woke in undertone. And we are reaping the results.

We tend to believe that an organization can lose its soul. And we know this is a bad thing. A building can be soulless, and we don't want to live there. We know exactly what we mean when we say, 'he sold his soul' and have witnessed the devasting aftermath of those kinds of transactions. We instinctively know searching one's soul is to look in a deeper place, in search of something better. But we don't talk much about the essential influence that comes from this deepest of places. The best of leaders digs down, tends and keeps that place healthy, and then leads from there. From a well-watered soul. I call this 'soul leadership'.

We could just call it 'leadership', but we would miss something essential in doing so. The very mystique of soul, the enigmatic quality, forces us to dig – and that's the point. You have to dig deep for it. Soul is the foundation of 'the project'. All you lead, all you build, starts there. From your soul. As long as you allow it, and acknowledge it, and tend it.

RECOVERING THE SOUL

Of course, the thing about foundations is that people don't really care about them until they fail and whatever you made slides or subsides, crumbles or collapses.

Recently, I found myself in a pretty dark place. I had just left a role that I loved, leading an organization I had helped birth, which had grown significantly and made some remarkable impacts.

I had given more of myself to that organization than I probably should have. I knew leaving was the right move; I was asking some hard questions about the institution itself and I was stagnating as a leader. To be really honest, the organization I had founded was beginning to do so, too. So, I left. At the age of fifty-one, I began to pivot my life.

I was prepared for disappointment from some, for the speculation of others, and for questions as to the motive of this change. I hadn't lost my faith, wasn't reneging on my calling, and certainly didn't need to leave for any relational or moral reason. I was truly doing the right thing – for me, for them, it would be better for all – and yet change is always hard to embrace.

What I wasn't prepared for was the pain of misunderstanding from close friends and colleagues, those I'd worked alongside and sought to encourage over decades. It felt like abandonment and rejection and took me to a bleak corner in my mind. I had written books and run courses on leadership and had been regarded as a leader in the very subject area that was now under the microscope. The relational influence I had always enjoyed felt like the very area I'd failed. It devastated me.

As I took time to process, two equal and opposite reactions began to emerge in me. Both, I now know to be toxic.

First came the impulse to beat myself up. The internal narrative went like this: I was the leader, things didn't go the way I imagined they should, it's my fault. Entirely. Therefore, I'm not the leader I think I am, not fit for the leadership I thought I was, and I should stop trying to lead. Ever.

After I had sat for a while in the dust, with the worms, feeling useless and then a little sorry for myself, another equally strong emotion began to rise up in me. Indignation.

My narrative now acknowledged that I had not been treated well. That a story was being passed around that just wasn't true and that others were using for their own ends. When people we love break agreement with us, something breaks within us. I was determined not to defend myself, so when I was attacked, I stewed in solitude.

Neither one of these reactions was wholly right or completely wrong. But as I sat with these emotions, I realized that this moment – although not life and death for me – contained within it the potential to make or diminish me.

I thought I was on a journey to reboot my life; I was actually on a quest to find my soul again – I just didn't have the words for it at the time. I began to see that if this moment was to have any redemptive outcome, the only posture of value was to address all causes in myself. Not the self-flagellation of my first reaction, but a more measured and curious sense of seeking to understand more deeply how I'd contributed to the current state.

The problem, as I began to unpack it, was not in my mind. I understood the principles of leadership well. The problem was, equally, not in my heart. I loved people well. The problem was to do with soul. I had begun to lead and live from another place – not from a shallow place, but something had been lost. It wasn't initially obvious, to me or anyone else. It wasn't intentional. It was accidental.

And that was the problem. If you don't fight to lead from your soul, you won't. You'll react, rather than respond. You'll deal with the urgent and neglect the important. You'll leave no margin to reconnect with your essence and purpose. Everything around you will conspire to draw everything within you to lead from a lesser place. You'll find yourself soulless. I hadn't come close to selling my soul, but I might have misplaced it, somewhere in the middle of trying to do things. Mostly good things.

Our leadership problems are most often found in the soul. They're most often solved there, too. You must do all you can to find your soul if you want to lead well. This is hard stuff, not only because it is hard to conceptualize and materialize, but it's also challenging to measure. And yet, we know it's possible; we know leadership of this kind does exist. It is rare, but it exists.

Much is being spoken, written, and advocated about self-care and how to prioritize your mental and physical well-being. These practices might well be soul-care. I have sought to define what the soul is; the question becomes how can we care for it effectively?

George Fuechsel, an early IBM programmer and trainer, popularized the acronym GIGO to describe the limitations and the power of a machine: Garbage In Garbage Out![4] I'd like to offer up an alternative to describe the limitations and power of a leader: HIHO. Health In Health Out.

What is *in*, is what will *out*. The project is you. Not your skills (not firstly). Not your strategies. Not the newest idea from the latest leadership playbook. Not your doings … but your being. This is a book about you – and about you making some commitments. Some agreements with yourself.

In my own dark place, I discovered something that I now understand to be the key for cultivating leadership and leading from a place of soul; I unearthed four characteristics that I want to be the legacy of my ongoing leadership; traits that come from my soul and cannot be attained unless I intentionally excavate and mine them from deep within myself. I have determined to make agreements with myself and I challenge you to do the same.

Agreements to be the leader you could be and to lead others to the same end. Agreements to be:

TRUE and to provoke authentic and integrous leadership in others

BRAVE and to encourage courageous and focused leadership in those around you

4 William Lidwell, Kritina Holden, and Jill Butler, *Universal Principles of Design, Revised and Updated: 125 Ways to Enhance Usability, Influence Perception, Increase Appeal, Make Better Design Decisions, and Teach through Design* (Rockport Publishers, 2010), p112.

KIND and to spread that connected kindness so that it is caught by leaders who follow you

CURIOUS and to catalyze creativity and growth in all those who look to you to lead them

Even as you read, as you stand in the circle (which we talked about earlier in 'The Project'), as you become the project, I'm going to ask you to make an agreement to make these agreements.

These qualities, we will discover, are found and forged in practices, in a rhythm, in some deeper places:

THE CAVE: The quest of the True

THE ROAD: The way of the Brave

THE TABLE: The art of the Kind

THE FIRE: The pursuit of the Curious

Habitually.

And as you live these agreements, I'm going to ask you to begin to practise this rhythm. This intentional rhythm – borrowed from my Celtic heritage, practised, and proven over centuries by those who led from a deeper place – is offered to empower a different quality of leader.

The Cave, the Road, the Table and the Fire is a pattern for your project, a beat for your days. Not a rhythm you have to march to. But a groove you can find. Leaders who find this kind of groove have a competitive advantage. They own the future. I know this is difficult stuff, but stay with me.

Draw a circle
Take responsibility
Make agreements
Keep agreements
Find your groove

In this book we will consider what it means to lead from your soul. Not from value statements or playbooks, but from a deeper place, from the core of who you really are. And we will consider how to care for and maintain that place.

This is not a book for the fainthearted. It is, of course, written to be read. But it is also written to be marked up and underlined. It is written to provoke, equip and to be disagreed with. It must, in parts, be disagreed with. If you find nothing to disagree with, I probably haven't done my job.

Nor is it reserved only for those graced with particular personality types, leadership styles and privileged backstories. The agreements are birthright for all of us and the spaces are available to any who want them enough.

This is for you. And then it is for them. *All* of them – those who will be impacted by your leadership.

You are the project.

It's just four words, but it might just be a life sentence.
It's just four letters, and it just might be the point of the project.

HIHO.

CHAPTER 1

AN ETCHING

FIXING THE CHARACTER OF OUR TIMES

I sank deep into an antique armchair (probably a Howard and Sons) by the open fire and picked up my journal. This library, in an unspoilt English stately home, was almost certainly the very room where William Wilberforce had gathered with his Clapham Sect[5] to dream, to conspire, and to work tirelessly, year after year, towards the abolition of slavery.

That evening, I shared this historic reading room with remarkable men and women – leaders of emerging talent. They were would-be politicians, early-days business leaders and gifted writers. So much potential in such a portentous room.

On the one hand, there was little unusual about gathering a group of next generation leaders, as Niki, my wife, and I have been trying to prioritize these moments all our lives. But on the other, there was something uncommonly pertinent about the moment, the hunger and the space.

We'd been exploring the power of influence. As we reflected on what we'd learned, breathing in the atmosphere of ancient leather, woodsmoke and whisky, we talked of a different kind of leadership.

The fire cracked and sighed, the Lagavulin 16 glowing in the heavy crystal tumblers, and Rob (at twenty-three, already the veteran of two start-ups), fresh from his first significant failure and in the throes of debt and the fear of redundancies, murmured:

5 Stephen Tomkins, *The Clapham Sect: How Wilberforce's Circle Transformed Britain* (Lion Hudson, 2010).

'What kind of leader is that? What kind of leader is it who "fixes the character of their times"?'

A pause. We all recognized the allusion. I had referenced it earlier in the day – an inscription in the north choir aisle of Westminster Abbey, a tribute to a remarkable leader. A leader who had changed the way things were.

To the memory of William Wilberforce (born in Hull August 24th 1759, died in London July 29th 1833); for nearly half a century a member of the House of Commons, and, for six parliaments during that period, one of the two representatives for Yorkshire. In an age and country fertile in great and good men, he was among the foremost of those who fixed the character of their times.[6]

The memorial goes on to talk specifically about Wilberforce's involvement in the abolition of slavery and his leadership of culture at the time.

'Don't forget,' countered Alice, *'there was nothing perfect about the record or character of Wilberforce, or any of the "great and good men" – or indeed, women – that the country was then fertile with. Wilberforce opposed some reforms which would have seriously relieved poverty. There is much that might be questioned about the philosophies and practices of many of these privileged people.'*

It was the kind of comment that Alice often made, justice-conscious as she was, always provocative, sometimes right.

'No doubt,' continued Rob, *'Wilberforce was flawed. But to make the slightest impression, the least dent on your culture, to*

6 Westminster Abbey, 'William Wilberforce & family', Westminster-abbey.org (accessed 10 August 2023).

have someone remember your name beyond your generation is a huge thing. And to "fix the character of your times"? That seems monumental, like another order of huge.'

I jumped in, grasping the moment to suggest that, at that time 'fix' didn't mean 'mend' – it didn't mean to put a new screw in a door hinge, or a drop of WD40 to solve an annoying squeak. The word has come to mean a temporary mend: the supergluing of a broken mug handle. But when the memorial was engraved, 'fix' probably meant something more like 'to set'. To set the character of our times.

I couldn't have planned the evening better if I tried. The fire was playing its part. As the flames danced, our minds turning over the ideas and events of the day, we went deeper. Alice had put aside her prejudice and this was the moment to make the salient point. I spoke again:

'That's exactly what great leadership does. All the time. The character of leadership sets the character of society. As it is in the character of leaders, so it is in the characteristics of our culture. Any culture, any business environment, any public office or any family. As it is with the leader, so it goes for everything the other side of that leader. It takes character to fix character.'

I leafed back in my journal to a note I'd written earlier.

'The word "character" comes from the Greek "kharakter," which means a stamping tool.[7] It came to describe the mark left on a coin during its manufacture. It describes an etching or something that is deeply embedded.'

7 John Frow, *Character & Person* (Oxford University Press, 2014), pp7, 248.

An embedding of character. An etching of the soul. Somehow, in the dimly lit room, it felt as if we'd meandered into one of the most significant conversations any of us could have. On the character of leadership and how it is formed. On the quality of culture and how it is tended. On where these two concepts are linked and whether they could ever be 'fixed'. And if any of us could lead in such a way that would have lasting, etched impact.

And as we talked later into the night, feeding the fire at various lulls, it became clear, at least to those in the room that perhaps never had this conversation been more needed or relevant.

Let's step away from that room for a while to try to understand our leadership moment, at least a little.

VUCA

Volatile, Uncertain, Complex and Ambiguous. VUCA was a term used by leadership experts Warren Bennis and Burt Nanus in their book, *Leaders: Strategies for Taking Charge*,[8] to describe the context of the US Army War College's response to the ending of the Cold War. Bennis and Nanus point out that this term can be aptly applied to the challenges facing strategic leadership of all kinds in every arena of culture since.

What Bennis and Nanus anticipated was the instability of a deeply confused world that could comprehensively destroy itself in the rise of a rogue nation or a terrorist cause by the press of a button. They almost certainly didn't have the data set to imagine a civilization run largely by Artificial Intelligence and all the terrifying implications of that possibility. Or the growing body of evidence that our ecosystems have become untenable, and that our planet itself is now subject to unsustainable forces likely to destroy

8 Warren G Bennis and Burt Nanus, *Leaders: Strategies for Taking Charge* (Harper Business, 2007).

it. When Bennis and Nanus shared the term VUCA the world had little appreciation of the power of a world wide web – or the far-reaching societal changes that would follow, for good or ill. Nor had they just experienced a Covid-19 pandemic that put life as we know it on pause, and placed an already beleaguered leadership in the spotlight as never before.

If they were writing now, the 'A' trait in VUCA might be described as 'anxious' or 'angry' instead of 'ambiguous'. What is clear is that leadership in this VUCA world is under more pressure and greater scrutiny than it has ever been. And that, more than ever, we need clarity to arise amidst ambiguity; simplicity amidst complexity; stability amidst undertainty and peace amidst volatility.

This will take a 'fixing'. Not only will this require a different quality of leadership, it's going to need to come from a deeper place – deeper spaces. A better approach toward leadership as a whole.

When French conservative thinker Joseph de Maistre observed that, 'Every nation gets the government it deserves,'[9] he was making a statement about the nature of democracy. But he might as well have been making a statement about the conditions we create for leadership. We get the leaders we deserve.

We might well argue that not only is our context VUCA but our attempts at leading our way through it is VUCA, as well. We appear to be stuck in a cycle – an understandable but sabotaging pattern that undermines the very leadership we need. A cycle repeated over time. We deify, then we demonize, then we deny.

Deify: We raise up leaders, expecting much of them, then take a ringside seat and watch them fail to meet our unrealistic expectations and their overreaching claims. As leaders, we collude by believing our own press, or even creating it! Feeding our minor messiah complexes.

9 Richard J. Ellis and Michael Nelson, *Debating Reform: Conflicting Perspectives on How to Fix the American Political System* (CQ Press, 2020), p101.

Demonize: We respond to failures of leadership by tearing down the very same people we wildly promoted. Eagerly citing all that is wrong in them and discrediting even that which is good. We gossip about and deride those we once followed. As leaders, we can so easily believe *we are* the failure we've experienced; our inability to separate our personhood from our position takes us down.

Deny: Consequently, we blame the office of leadership or at least become deeply cynical of anyone who chooses to take responsibility. We then fail to teach leadership as of primary importance, and the resultant 'leadership phobia' means we sabotage even our own leadership potential. Good people with great ideas and strong character then run a million miles away from formal leadership.

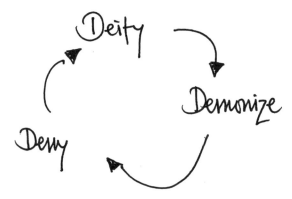

And we end up with the leaders we deserve.

Our society does this on repeat. What is more, the opportunity our social media-obsessed world affords us to do this is unparalleled. Maybe the problem is not more pervasive today, just more public. None of us are purely victims in this populist farce. In fact, we create, enjoy, endure and then perpetuate it.

This moment is a circle moment. We owe ourselves, and those who come after us, a different conversation about leadership – a better conversation about leadership. The old models seem defunct and the current solutions deficient. But the right response can't be to simply blame leadership as a concept; to cancel it, resign from it, to leave it broken for someone else to fix. We get the leaders we deserve and the culture that is the overspill of them. We become the leaders we choose to become. The problem is more complex than it has ever been; could the solution be as simple as it's always been?

Back to the library . . .

'Those who penned the original tribute to Wilberforce deliberately used the word character as the descriptor. They might have understood it to be an etching of the soul,'

'We might not use those specific words, and yet we know implicitly that great leadership comes from a deeper place. It owes less to tactics, policies and models and far more to qualities like integrity, honesty, resilience, dependability, bravery and humility. These are core to you – your character.

'What if the essence of you, the soul of you, could determine the impact of you? And that you can train that soul, tend that soul, so its health flows from you to those around you; could that fix the character of the times?'

I left them with that thought. We moved from the library to our respective rooms, conversations paused for another day.

Perhaps for *this* day. *This* conversation.

Sit with me – let's poke the fire and drink this in. Your soul can become etched with the kind of qualities that fix the character of our times.

John's got it. We'll call him John, it's not his real name. I think we all have a John or a Jane in our minds – or they might be an amalgamation of the Johns and Janes we know. You might have met them in parts, in different people. Your John. Your Jane.

My John is grounded and centred – not in an arrogant way, but in a way that makes you feel more at peace when he is there. At ease in boardrooms, in company and at home with himself. When he talks to you, he's truly interested in you and nothing else seems to matter. When he speaks about the things he's passionate about, he moves the dial, he changes atmospheres and he wins the room. When he decides he does so wisely, definitively and effectively. When he brings about change, he does so kindly. There is something about John. People love to be around him. Leaders want to follow him.

Jane has it, too. She isn't perfect – and she's not trying to pretend she is. She has weaknesses, she's working on some and celebrating others. Jane looks after herself – body, mind and spirit – but lives with others in mind. When Jane's life is torpedoed by the kind of thing that does that to lives – sickness, loss, rejection (you could add to the list) – she more than survives, she thrives. Jane gathers people and they follow gladly. In truth she has that almost unnatural ability to turn life's losses to wins, not just for herself, but for her people as well.

You might not know what to call it or be able to put your finger on it. But you've seen it in them and you want it for you. It's a deeply attractive thing. It fixes things, it sets things and it changes things.

What is it that makes these Johns and Janes? We may have known more driven leaders with bigger acclaim, greater wealth and more letters after their names. We probably know better dressers with sharper haircuts. But John and Jane carry themselves well. There is a grace and a pace to life that is almost grooved. It leaves a mark, indelibly, like a stamping tool. It changes things, for the good. People want to be around this life. I want to be around this life. We all want this to be *our* life.

And I asked myself, what is the secret to such a life?

And the only answer I could muster was an etching of the soul.

CHAPTER 2

CADENT

Blackpool
Brighton
Southend-on-Sea

Traditional British seaside towns conjure a picture of drizzly summer holidays. Of stripey wind breaks, donkey rides, sandy homemade sandwiches eaten swiftly between the summer squalls.

And rock. Rock is a very British phenomenon. A stick of sugar, sticky and sweet, pink and white, designed to be licked and crunched and terrible for your teeth. The unique characteristic of a stick of seaside rock is that the name of whatever town you bought it in is written indelibly through the middle of it. Wherever you bite it, it spells wherever you are.

Soul is much like that stick of rock. An etching of the soul happens over time – it's grooved and grown. If it's not deep in you, cut through you, it can never flow from you to those you lead around you.

The project must become a pattern. Or it will never become permanent. It has to run right through you. Or it is not really true of you. The real you must bleed from you. It's not just that you show up honestly as who you are, it's that you *always* do. It's the same for all of the soul agreements. Bravery must run in you, be the default for you, all through you, if Soul Leadership is going to flow from you. If kindness is not your natural response and curiosity not consistent for you, you are not tending to and leading from that deepest place.

Soul leadership must be integral. It must be fractal.

In 1975, IBM research professor Benoit Mandelbrot, a Polish-born American mathematician, revealed to the world a concept he called 'fractal geometry,'[10] which essentially described a never-ending pattern – the dynamic integration of the same complex pattern within the pattern seen infinitely. No matter which way you look at it or where you cut it, the exact same pattern is visible.

It's beyond the rock phenomenon.

If you've ever studied a snowflake, you have seen a fractal. Or cut into a stem of broccoli – a big broccoli floret is made up of small broccoli florets. The micro mirrors the macro. Within these repeated patterns, the big picture is formed from the little picture. You can see it in trees. Or pineapples. Or organizations.

Repeated cultural patterns run through most organizations. The small interactions reflect the bigger values. Sit in the restaurant or coffee shop of the company you work for do it over several days and watch for consistent patterns and know that how you are being treated is what you can expect to encounter in the boardroom.

Pay close attention to any materials you are handed at a reception desk or artifacts you observe in the lobby. Look for consistent patterns and fully expect their content and quality to be your experience throughout your interactions with the business.

Soul is a fractal system. A stick of rock. It's consistent. Etched. Over time. An infinitely repeating pattern.

THE CAVE, THE ROAD, THE TABLE AND THE FIRE

In recent years a great deal of attention has been given to the importance of self-care – caring for our mental and physical well-being. The well-being of our soul is equally vital; these practices might well be soul-care.

If True, Brave, Kind and Curious are the qualities that are the mark of healthy Soul Leadership, the Cave, the Road, the Table and

10 Benoit B. Mandelbrot, *The Fractal Geometry of Nature* (Echo Point Books & Media, 2021).

the Fire are the spaces and practices for the forming and tending of that leadership.

Let me make it more personal. Your current intentions, habits and performance determine your present leadership and ALL future outcomes. Whether your thing is coding or free kicks, sketching or scales, public speaking or private negotiation, you will never perform at optimum until it is engrained in you and grooved in your muscle memory.

Leading from your soul comes the same way. It's all about pattern or rhythm.

RHYTHM

I have never met anyone I admire as a leader who doesn't have an intentional cadence to their days, their seasons, for their lives. Think about it. Think about them.

I have also met and coached hundreds of leaders who have resisted the need to develop patterns for their lives and have let rhythm happen to them. It is no wonder so many live discordant leadership lives and feel they are always off the pace, out of time or striving for something they never become.

These leaders might be ambitious goal setters, planners, New Year's resolution makers, but equally often they are failed-to-follow-through-ers, not because they didn't intend to, but because they didn't establish a rhythm and they quickly lost the cadence. Then the point.

Living cadent is not an optional extra for a soulful life. It is the way of the soulful life. It is a showing up, a having a go, practising hard, processing deeply, daily, repeatedly and habitually, until there is a groove.

This grooving comes rhythmically. The challenge might be that what is natural for us is not the way we actually live out our lives.

There is rhythm in you – it's already in there. After all, this world we inhabit has rhythm. Creation is cadent. The sun rises and sets. The tides rise and fall. The seasons come and go – winter, spring, summer and autumn (or 'fall', if you must). The body you carry around owes all to rhythm. Your mother's heartbeat is almost certainly the first sound you hear. Your heartbeat is the first rhythm you receive, and every day after, the most important noise in your world. An unstressed short sound followed by a stressed longer sound.

Each day your heart beats around 100,000 times and pumps in perfect cadence 2,000 gallons of blood around the body.[11] If your heart ceases to beat, or your lungs fail to reflate, you'll cease to be.

As it goes for that rhythm, so it goes for you. Your body is designed to be worn in rhythm – circadian rhythm, to be more precise. The internal clock regulating our energy levels shapes our entire physical and emotional world. These rhythms govern our sleep and wake cycles, and are influenced by light and dark and seasonal change, and interrupting or disturbing them has been linked to a huge raft of medical ailments and conditions.

So, pretty important then.

And how we learn and what we remember and what we treasure owes much to rhythm.

The first bedtime stories I read my girls had a pattern, a cadence, that made them easy to listen to, remember and repeat.

11 Sian E. Harding, *The Exquisite Machine: The New Science of the Heart* (The MIT Press, 2022), p4.

We can't go over it.
We can't go under it.
Oh no!
We've got to go through it.[12]

And although the brain becomes more sophisticated, as we mature, the human mind never gets beyond a primal predisposition to rhythm. Perhaps that's why all the English literature quotations I can ever recall were written in iambic pentameter.

If music be the food of love play on … [13]

But soft what light from yonder window breaks … [14]

And while I can't remember where I left my keys or phone, I can recall the lyrics to hundreds of songs from the eighties and nineties. The power of rhythm still surprises me. The rousing effect of the pipes and drums at the Edinburgh Tattoo and the lump in my throat and the quickly hidden tear in my eye. The pacifying effect of rocking a baby to sleep. Rhythm regulates mood and changes the way we behave.[15]

The truth is that we were made to live cadent, and yet, we settle for erratic or discordant and wonder why we feel exhausted. Out of whack. Tetchy. Dissatisfied. And what even is a soul?

CANUTE WAS RIGHT AND SO WAS EDISON

At school I learned the story of King Canute,[16] the legendary King of Britain who, thinking he had power over nature, instructed his courtiers to carry him down to the sea so he could forbid the tide from coming in.

12 Michael Rosen and Helen Oxenbury, *We're Going on a Bear Hunt* (Little Simon, 1997).
13 William Shakespeare, *Twelfth Night* (Wordsworth Editions Ltd, 1997), p13.
14 William Shakespeare, *Romeo and Juliet* (Arden Shakespeare, 2000), p62.
15 Deb Dana, *Polyvagal Theory in Therapy* (W.W. Norton & Company, 2018), pp152–153.
16 Timothy Bolton, *Cnut the Great* The English Monarch Series (Yale University Press, 2019).

The moral of the story was 'don't be foolish like Canute; there are many things in life you have no control over; don't try to control them.' It turns out that in the original version of the story, King Canute is attempting to show his weakness, not his power. In fact, he is not being foolish, he is being wise. 'See how we try to control the very things we have no control over!'

The moral of the tale, whichever way you tell it, stands the test of time. If you live a life trying to defy the elements, ignoring or setting yourself against the natural rhythms it will be hard, unnatural (not surprisingly) and will rarely turn out well in the end.

You can't control nature – you just can't.

And yet we try. All the time. We call this trying 'progress'. And celebrate it.

As I was growing up, I was regularly inspired by another story from the life of Thomas Edison, perhaps the greatest inventor of the modern age. Edison developed a practical light bulb in his laboratory in Menlo Park, NJ. I was told Edison tried over 1,000 times to get the invention right.

Once again, the numbers in the story might not be wholly accurate, but the point is that after more than 3,000 designs for bulbs between 1878 and 1880, Edison presented the world with a light that seemed at first glance to bring into question Canute's wisdom. Now you *can* defy the laws of nature and stretch the hours of daylight and change the way you work and rest and play and relate.

And we have been doing it ever since and calling it good. Or 'progress.'

And then Tim Berners-Lee, in 1989, invented the World Wide Web,[17] and over the last few decades, we have become experts at the bending of time, the shrinking of distances and the almost infinite

17 Walter Isaacson, *The Innovators: How a Group of Hackers, Geniuses, and Geeks Created the Digital Revolution* (Simon & Schuster, 2015), pp412–429.

expansion of opportunities. The internet has made it possible to work at any hour from almost any location and connect with almost anywhere and anyone.

And stop the tide. At any time of day or night. (Or not.)

And it is good. (Sometimes.)

It is increasingly hard to find rhythm and almost normal to live 'out of sorts' with the world around us and with ourselves. Our bodies and minds are designed to be aligned with the world we inhabit, and yet, the patterns we've adopted are in conflict with it. And we wonder why we carry a deep sense that something feels off.

Perhaps our rhythm might be 'off'. Our cadence might also be 'off'. And this current age might just be suffering from a severe case of collective cognitive dissonance.

Edison and Canute could both offer something here. We don't want to be slaves to the elements in their extremes. But we mustn't ignore them either. And ultimately we can't control them.

So we listen to all those podcasts, chugging black coffee, on the way to the office or dropping our kids at school. We deep breathe in the morning after drinking three pints of water and do hot yoga on the way home from work. Because we want to live authentically and healthily in this fast-changing world and not 'lose our souls'. And then just give up.

FINDING BALANCE OR GETTING IN THE ZONE?

I can't tell you the number of times a well-meaning parent, mentor or friend has encouraged me to 'find balance' as the answer to whatever challenge or stress I was facing at that particular moment.

I will tell you that it's very often that I encourage myself to 'get in the zone' on the golf course, at least once a round. I have spent years watching sportsmen and women 'in the zone' and my favourite musicians find their 'groove', some magical mystical zen-like state of almost perfection. I have tried to copy and failed to match. And these attempts just seemed to create more challenge and greater stress. Maybe I'm doing it wrong? Or, maybe balance or flow isn't the place to start or even the *whole* answer.

You don't get balance by trying to be balanced, nor do you get 'in the flow' by attempting to flow. It all comes a different way.

THE LIMITATIONS OF BALANCE

For years, the received wisdom has been to aim for a work/life balance. The actual term 'work/life balance' first appeared in the late 1970s as a key part of the Women's Liberation Movement, used to highlight the inequalities in opportunity and the prospective imbalance of a working woman's life.[18] More recently, it has been the go-to ambition to counter the stresses of overwork for the modern employee.

It's a noble goal. But probably always just out of reach. For anyone whose job is their calling, whose home is their office, or who runs a family business, the lines are so blurred that it's seriously challenging to work out where work ends and life begins. Full-time life? Part-time work? Spare time? No time!

The problem is not balance. It might be an overestimation of its effect in dealing with our clumsy attempts at soul, as if this golden bullet called 'balance' is a fix-all for our post-modern leadership lives. More likely, it's that we are approaching balance as if it is a static state we can reach or achieve. Balance, rather, might be a moving target – in fact, that may well be the whole point. You could be trying to find it in all the wrong ways.

Let's look at balance. If we could travel back in time 4,000 years to the Indus valley, which is modern day Pakistan, we would

18 Kathi Weeks, *The Problem with Work: Feminism, Marxism, Antiwork Politics, and Postwork Imaginaries,* a John Hope Franklin Center Book (Duke University Press, 2011), p110.

be there at the invention of this concept we call balance.[19] Our entrepreneurial forefathers needed to find a way to measure the worth of produce so they could trade. The 'balance scale' came into being. Two flat surfaces connected by a beam and poised on a central pivot. Produce was placed on one side and weighing stones on the other to measure the worth of the goods. It was a huge leap forward in humanity's ability to civilize.

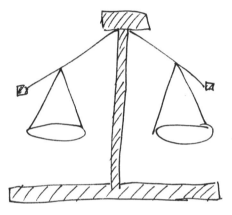

Sometime later, thinkers and philosophers, Aristotle being prominent among them, caught onto the idea that as balance of physical items had been a catalyst for economic and societal advance, it might be that balance as a philosophical concept had wider applications.[20] Could humanity's ability to build relationships, engage in geo-politics and navigate increasingly complex lives depend largely on our understanding of balance?

They reasoned 'yes' and they were right.

Partly.

19 Karl M. Petruso, *Early Weights and Weighing in Egypt and the Indus Valley*, Volume 79 (Boston MFA Bulletin, 1981), pp44–51.
20 Joel Kaye, *A History of Balance, 1250–1375: The Emergence of a New Model of Equilibrium and its Impact on Thoughts* (Cambridge University Press, 2016) pp90–92.

You see, it's one thing when what is being measured is a bag of wheat on a wood and metal construction. It's altogether another when what is being weighed is the whole of life. Humanity has proved over many centuries that you don't get balance by trying to be balanced. At least not perfectly and certainly not on its own. In fact, trying to be balanced will often make you more likely to fall.

Have you noticed the Lycra-clad cycle guy at the traffic light? The one who doesn't want to unclip from his pedals? He adjusts and wobbles and looks like he is one small gust of wind or a sudden blast of a horn away from humiliation and disaster, notwithstanding the truth that nobody over the age of forty should ever wear full Lycra.

The fact is, balance, applied on its own, is tentative, vulnerable and temporary.

Now watch the cyclist as the lights go green and he speeds away down the hill – no wobble, no danger, just fluent stability. It is amazing how quickly and easily balance follows movement in rhythm. Or think of a marathon runner, taking each step at just the right length and speed, completely comfortable in her stride. Or the way a set of musical chords is played with the perfect touch and tempo and rhythm together. Balance and movement in rhythm, working together. It's a thing called cadence.

Cadence is king. Pursue cadence, balance and productivity will follow.

A FIXATION WITH FLOW

In the late 1970s and early 1980s, Hungarian positive psychologist Mihaly Csikszentmihalyi recognized a state he called 'flow':

> A state in which people are so involved in an activity that nothing else seems to matter; the experience is so enjoyable that people will continue to do it even at great cost, for the sheer sake of doing it.[21]

21 Mihaly Csikszentmihalyi, *Flow: The Psychology of Optimal Experience* (Harper Perennial Modern Classics, 2008), p4.

He studied thousands of subjects over many years, from artists to composers to tradesmen, trying to discover what made people great and happy. Csikszentmihalyi employed an experience sampling method, giving his subjects pagers (for those born after 1995, Google it). They were asked to answer a series of questions about their feelings whenever their pagers beeped. What he discovered was a mental state of operation that people inhabited for brief periods, during which they could perform an activity in optimum energy focus. They found their zone and achieved their best.

A ten-year McKinsey study into flow[22] concluded that top executives reported being five times more productive in flow state, which means they could basically get a week's worth of work done in one day. Not only does flow impact productivity, but also skill and precision. Military snipers improved their target acquisition skills by 230% when they were induced into a flow state artificially.[23]

When you flow, your own success transcends your effort and you become better than you ever imagined. For a moment you find your sweet spot. It's the most remarkable experience. I've felt it when speaking to a crowd, and everyone is connected to the point and held in the moment. It feels almost like time has stood still. Or a 3-iron hit flush, out of the middle, with just the right penetration through the air – it flies and lands and checks next to the hole. (This is mostly a figment of my imagination.)

Take a few seconds now to think of your own examples, your own moments. Moments when it has felt like you are doing what you were made to do, as only you can.

These transcendent moments are not possible all the time. They might not even be optimal all the time – being too focused on flow could lead to missing out on the richness of all that is not flow, valuable for learning, mourning, empathy and discovery.

22 McKinsey & Company, 'The Flow Effect: How to Achieve High Performance Under Pressure,' in *Harvard Business Review*, July–August 2021, pp89-97.
23 Steven Kotler, *The Rise of Superman: Decoding the Science of Ultimate Human Performance* (Penguin Random House, 2014), p218.

That said, I want more flow. I suspect you do too.

But you don't find flow by striving to find flow. At least not that often. It comes as overflow.

Flow is an overflow of cadence.

18·29 M

18.29M, 60FT.

The 1995 athletics world championships were held in Gothenburg, Sweden. On a balmy August evening, Jonathan Edwards triple jumped into history.[24] He jumped further than anyone ever: 18.29m (60ft). On that night, he increased his own world record by 31cm, a mark that, almost thirty years later, still stands.

The numbers are important, as they always are, but the way those numbers were achieved – what it looked like, felt like and represented – is far more important. In that moment, Edwards transcended athletics.

A mesmeric moment of flow, a study in balance and poise, when everything seems to be right, when time appears to stand still. Just like the perfect stone, skimmed at the perfect angle, with the optimum spin, across the stillest millpond. The achievement confirmed the effort.

Later, he casually noted that, 'it's only jumping into a sandpit,' and yet, this was way more than power, spikes, self-talk and tiny shorts.

The record and this gold medal were achieved by cadence. And not just the cadence of the hop, skip and jump, but the pattern of days, of a life lived rhythmically in service of moments of flow.

I suspect that most of us will never try to break an athletics world record, but you can find balance and you will experience flow – it's on the far side of cadence.

24 Rob Woodgate, *Jonathan Edwards: The Greatest Triple Jumper of All Time* (Mainstream Publishing, 2002).

CADENCE IS THE FORCE MULTIPLIER

Cadence is what will get you balance – it's the gateway to flow and what will make your Soul Leadership fractal. Cadence is the pattern and practice that will etch you with soul. That cadence must be simple, so you can do it. Daily. And it must be sticky, so you remember to do it. Daily.

This is the way I find cadence:

The Cave
The Road
The Table
The Fire

THE PROJECT IS SPATIAL

If you want to grow in knowledge you might go to a university or a library; physical fitness might be honed in a gym. If you are pursuing spiritual wisdom, you are likely to seek a place of worship. Where mental health is a challenge, a retreat centre or a clinic might be the location.

If you want to learn to lead yourself; to sit in that circle, to fix your character and the character of your time; if you want to learn to lead from a deeper place – from your soul – there are places to work on that too. These are places many of us go to anyway each day. You may have a Cave. You set out on a Road every day. You sit at your Table and reflect at a Fire.

But if your Cave is your morning social-media fix, your Road a job you hate, if your Table is a stool in a fast-food restaurant and your Fire the TV screen, will you get to where you hope to be?

And if you rush through these places, distracted, or stumble aimlessly, will you become who you want to be?

Read on ...

>

THE ROAD

⊼

THE TABLE

△

THE FIRE

THE CAVE

CHAPTER 3

THE CAVE:
the quest of the True

In the calmness of the morning, before the mind is heated and weary by the turmoil of the day, you have a season of unusual importance for communing with God and yourself.

WILLIAM WILBERFORCE[25]

Meditation is about getting still enough to know the difference between the voice and you.

OPRAH WINFREY[26]

There lies a den
Beyond the seeming confines of the space
Made for the soul to wander in and trace
Its own existence

JOHN KEATS[27]

There is a little cavern here, by the side of a wide meadow, which has been a part of me any time these twelve years – or more.

LETTER FROM ROBERT LOUIS STEVENSON TO FANNY SITWELL[28]

25 Gordon MacDonald, *The Road We Must Travel: A Personal Guide for Your Journey* (Worthy Books, 2014)
26 Oprah Winfrey, *The Path Made Clear: Discovering Your Life's Direction and Purpose* (Flatiron Books, 2014), p102.
27 John Keats, *Complete Poems and Selected Letters of John Keats* (Modern Library, 2001), p168.
28 Bradford A. Booth and Ernest Mehew, ed., *The Letters of Robert Louis Stevenson*, vol ii (Yale University Press, 1995), p112.

As we passed the two-pointed hill, we could see the black mouth of Ben Gunn's cave and a figure standing by it, leaning on a musket … A gentle slope ran up from the beach to the entrance of the cave. At the top, the squire met us. To me he was cordial and kind, saying nothing of my escapade either in the way of blame or praise.

… And thereupon we all entered the cave. It was a large, airy place, with a little spring and a pool of clear water, overhung with ferns. The floor was sand. Before a big fire lay Captain Smollett; and in a far corner, only duskily flickered over by the blaze, I beheld great heaps of coin and quadrilaterals built of bars of gold. That was Flint's treasure that we had come so far to seek and that had cost already the lives of seventeen men from the *Hispaniola*. How many it had cost in the amassing, what blood and sorrow, what good ships scuttled on the deep, what brave men walking the plank blindfold, what shot of cannon, what shame and lies and cruelty, perhaps no man alive could tell. Yet there were still three upon that island – Silver, and old Morgan, and Ben Gunn – who had each taken his share in these crimes, as each had hoped in vain to share in the reward.

TREASURE ISLAND[29]

The cave of Ben Gunn in *Treasure Island*, where the marooned sailor hid dried goat meat and obsessed about cheese, was said to be inspired by a cave midway along an ancient road called the Darn Walk which hugs the River Allan, and connects the Scottish towns of Bridge of Allan and Dunblane.[30] Stevenson, who grew up in Edinburgh, came here many times in the 1860s with his parents on holiday and wrote fondly about the place in his journals and letters.

To choose the Cave as our first space may seem strange. Caves are for the most part damp and dark, inhospitable and uncomfortable places; the domain of bats and bears. And yet, for centuries, holy women and men, banished warriors, would-be statesmen

29 Robert Louis Stevenson, *Treasure Island* (Wordsworth Editions, 2018), p177.
30 Graham Balfour, *Robert Louis Stevenson: A Life*. 2 vols. (Methuen, 1901), p140.

and brilliant artists have all found caves to be honest spaces for introspective formation and launching pads for brave ventures.

The discipline of the Cave is, of course, not about a physical cave. My Cave is a chair in the corner near a window that looks onto the garden, accompanied by just the right levels of peace and disruption only nature itself can supply, and a fresh long black. This space is really about a going in, a sitting down, a taking time. More, it's about what you find in there.

It's about bumping into your true self, reminding yourself of your soul and setting yourself up for leadership. It's about finding treasure. First thing in the morning.

Mornings. I love that short moment of forgetfulness when first awake, the few seconds when the schedule that is impossibly tight, the unresolved 'to do' and the feedback from the boss are not yet remembered.

It would be, however, an unmitigated disaster if I were to head into the day and attempt to lead from that naïve mental standpoint. The first urgent email would consume the attention I should be giving to a priority project; a critical comment would have me questioning my own capability when I should be serving the team. The unintentional leader invariably becomes a victim of the unrelenting expectations of everybody else. Unprepared, you fall into the gravitational pull of your day. Your calendar will set you, your engagements direct you and your agreements all too easily become disagreements.

And yet, largely, that's what happens – it always does – when we don't intentionally get ahead of the day.

Canute, of course, was right. You will find it impossible to hold back the tide. But you can decide how you will enter the water. What you do or don't do at the start of the day sets the tone for the rest of the day.

So 'do' you – you in the Cave. Find space to fix your character. To find yourself. To remind yourself of what is True, so you don't begin lost and untrue. You might choose to pray, to meditate or to reflect, as I do. Or just take a moment to be aware of something greater, beyond the activity, the mundane, the process of the day ahead of you.

Our Celtic forefathers understood this. The monks, who established much of what we now call western civilization, understood that the intimate, still space offered a way to stand apart from the noise, demands and expectations of the world around and to set themselves towards whatever was most vital in the day ahead.[31]

In the highlands and islands of my homeland, there are monasteries and hermitages dotted around isolated headlands and inlets. Venturing further, you might discover, tucked between the hills and hidden in the ancient forests, the caves where the holy women and men came to be alone, with themselves, their thoughts and their God; it's where they fixed their character and culture.[32]

It is not only the ancients who practise the discipline of the Cave. There are more high-achievers who spend their first morning moments in some version of it than those who risk skipping it.

'I meditate every day. I do it in the mornings for about ten to fifteen minutes. I think it's important because it sets me up for the rest of the day, it's like having an anchor. If I don't do it, it feels like I'm constantly chasing the day, as opposed to being controlled and dictating the day.'[33]

That's the late Kobe Bryant speaking, one of the greatest basketball players of his or any other generation. The Cave is about taking a moment before all the other moments to set the inner narrative. You cannot control many of the things coming at you in any given day, but you can take responsibility for your perspective, your attitude and your responses. To an extent, how it goes for these things is

31 Christopher Dawson, *Religion and the Rise of Western Culture* (Hassel Street Press, 2021).
32 William Forbes Skene, *The Highlanders of Scotland* (Forgotten Books, 2018).
33 Kobe Bryant, 'The Power of Sleep and Meditation' posted 2020, Thrive video, 5:46.

dependent on whether you meet *you* in the Cave and what you talk about when you do.

In his book *Tribes: We Need You to Lead Us,* Seth Godin makes this seminal statement:

> People don't believe what you tell them.
> They rarely believe what you show them.
> They often believe what their friends tell them.
> They always believe what they tell themselves. [34]

We believe what we tell ourselves. Which means it is important that we take time to tell ourselves the truth in the morning. It will set the tone of our day. Of our week. Of our lives.

And other people believe what they tell themselves. Which also means for a leader to connect, to really lead, you must intercept *their* inner dialogue, get in the middle of the conversation they are having with themselves. You've got to read the context, the room, the characters and the moment in order to understand the objections, fears and hopes that are present. And then, speak directly to them.

When *you* are your audience, you need to do the same. What are you telling yourself? What do you want to tell yourself? Because what you believe is truth, to you, even when it might not be. It will direct your day, your team and your future.

So you must set yourself up to look for truth, for what is truly True, every morning. And if you don't, you won't lead with integrity. You won't lead from your soul.

Time in the Cave is not just important for your own mental well-being, but for the prospering of whatever enterprise you are currently undertaking. Your life – this day – will move in the direction of your thoughts. Your mind is the leader. In other words, if you want to live in any given day as you intend, in agreement with your agreements and in lockstep with soul, you will have to set

---

34 Seth Godin, *Tribes: We Need You to Lead Us* (Portfolio, 2008), p9.

yourself up for it. I want to be True, Brave, Kind and Curious, so I must enter into the Cave – daily.

The Cave is then, truly, a 'set-up'. Level with yourself, every morning, set yourself each day. Get in the way of your inner narrative and set it.

Your Cave, like mine, is probably not a cave. Your Cave might be a favourite chair with a coffee in a still-sleeping house, it might be your desk before colleagues arrive, or a makeup mirror where you prepare to face the day. Your Cave might be your seat on the train to work, noise-cancelling earbuds in place, or it might be the quiet of your car on the highway.

Wherever or whatever your Cave is, it needs to be a place of conversation. A place where you can be completely honest, completely you.

You with God, if you have a faith.

Or you with you. Your soul with yourself.

REWIRE YOUR MIND AND SET YOUR MOOD

Can you rewire your brain? Probably.[35]

Your brain is singular, remarkable and highly efficient. It is constantly looking for shortcuts and workarounds, ways to handle the incessant amount of information it must process. Conflicting ideas, multiple witnesses and almost unlimited options force the brain to operate not unlike a supercomputer. Your ability to hack your own brain relies on you understanding a little of how it works.

Your brain has two minds. We might describe them as the conscious and subconscious minds. Your conscious mind handles around 40 bits of data per second.[36] The sights, sounds, smells and experiences of your conscious world are far too complex and

---

35 Rick Hanson PhD, *Hardwiring Happiness: The New Brain Science of Contentment, Calm, and Confidence* (Harmony, 2016).
36 Bruce H. Lipton, *The Biology of Belief: Unleashing the Power of Consciousness, Matter & Miracles* (10th anniversary ed.), (Hay House, 2016), p82.

far too numerous for this mind to focus and process it all in a meaningful way.

At the same time, your subconscious mind can deal with so much more – over 40 million bits of data. In real time, your subconscious mind acts as a sponge in a constant state of receiving and filtering the information that it's being assaulted with. It will only send to the conscious mind what it's been trained to focus on, categorizing information in terms of relevance. All the irrelevant information is kept out of the conscious mind. The eye may see it, the ear may hear it, but the mind will not recognize it because it is considered irrelevant or not useful.

Two things are clear here:

1. The brain is looking for hacks. It's always listening, like a 'Super Siri,' noting your preferences, watching your focuses, and then editing the information it gives you. If social media companies could do it as well as your brain, we would all be even more worried than we are. It massages your options, narrows your choices, and offers you well-trod neural pathways to journey down. That's why your thoughts today are likely to be 95% the same as the thoughts you had yesterday.[37]

2. Intentionally or accidentally, you are setting and limiting your own focus and outcomes. The pathways your brain has set up for you are a set-up by you. You focus on what you have focused on. You see what you're predisposed to see. You get what you thought you would get.[38]

Pretty dark, huh? Pretty hopeless, too. Until you realize you have power to rewire your thinking, to redirect your brain, to set the

37 Attributed to Deepak Chopra. Mick Quinn, *The Uncommon Path of Awakening Authentic Joy* (O-Books, 2009), p154.
38 David Allen, *Getting Things Done: The Art of Stress-Free Productivity* (Penguin Books, 2015), p70.

focus, to get in the middle of the narrative and to show up at the world before it just shows up at you. We can rewire our own minds to set ourselves up for soul.

There is a small part of your brain called the Reticular Activation System,[39] or RAS for short. It's a small bundle of nerves at your brainstem which act as a filter.

The role of your RAS is to filter out unnecessary information, and filter in the most important information to get to your brain for processing. It goes on alert to find what you want – what *you've* told it to focus on. It will bring you what you've focused on in the past until you tell it differently.

It's why my girls have taken to calling me Karl. I try to reason with them. 'There are only four human beings on the planet who have the privilege of calling me "Dad" and none of you want to leverage it.' That line of argument, however compelling, never helps. They call me Karl, because whenever I am in a large crowd and they call me 'Dad,' I don't respond. My RAS filters out 'Dad,' but latches onto 'Karl'. The RAS takes what you focus on and creates a filter for it. Imperceptibly, it works without you knowing for better or worse. Pretty cool, huh?

But it also takes your beliefs and reinforces them. If you believe you can't do something, it reminds you constantly that what you believe is true; it limits your faith and therefore your practice.

What you think about you bring about. Think about that! Sobering, isn't it. What you focus on makes all the difference. Or, in the words of the Jedi Knight Qui-Gon Jinn,

39 Dawson Church, *Mind to Matter: The Astonishing Science of How Your Brain Creates Material Reality* (Hay House Inc, 2018), p104.

'Always remember, your focus determines your reality.'

GEORGE LUCAS, STAR WARS

So in the Cave, set your mind.

THREE SETTING QUESTIONS

The way your mind works means that your first conscious thought each day is never incidental; it is, in truth, formational and mustn't be accidental. This reality creates a significant challenge for us in a culture that is virulent, insistent and, unlike you, does not sleep.

The gravitational pull of this culture of production and performance is so powerful that unless you set up the day with some intentional thinking and curated questions, your soul will be drowned out with other perspectives.

If your day starts with a list with tick box options, you will subtly enthrone the activity of your day and there will likely be little room for any other aspect of humanity to gain a foothold, let alone be a priority. You will, as a consequence, find it hard to define your value by any other measure than production.

Equally, if you don't remind your soul of *what you are for* at the outset of the morning, how you behave will owe more to the clamouring of the zeitgeist around us than the soul agreements within us.

At the start, you need to fight for authenticity. In the Cave, ask yourself some simple, albeit significant, questions:

WHO AM I? What is the truth of me?

WHY AM I? What is the point of me?

HOW AM I? What is the experience of me?

And then the fourth and final question is *WHAT SHALL I DO?* When you answer this last, you create a space into which you can step with Truth, Bravery, Kindness and Curiosity. Every day you don't, it just remains a lottery.

Who am I?

Some of our closest friends have a beautiful, smart and strong-willed six-year-old daughter. She knows her own mind and is not shy in expressing it, often and loudly. Dad and Mum have encouraged her in a daily practice that they call her 'I am's.

'I am strong. I am loved. I am resourceful ... '

She is encouraged to speak out – and speak to herself – the qualities that, in her best moments, she wants to see in her life. She may be a little young yet – she still has meltdowns! She still doubts. But with the help of her parents, she is setting herself up to take a run at life, rather than just be steamrolled by it. She is learning to think and speak from her soul.

You should too.

Please don't hear what I'm not saying. I'm not asking you to yell into a mirror or to leave affirming sticky notes all around – although, if that's your thing, go for it! I'm just encouraging you to set perspective because it will set you up. For good or ill.

What I am saying is that I have seen these aspirational declarations changing the way we behave, re-wiring brains, transforming attitudes, confidences and then outcomes.

Reach for your own descriptor:

I am ...

Why Am I?

What is the point of me? What am I for today?

One of the obvious dangers of the pace of the world we inhabit is we can find ourselves 'doing' days of activity that bear little or no relationship to the lives we want to live or the legacies we desire to leave. Reminding myself of purpose ahead of activity is, at the very least, an attempt to bring meaning to action.

Purpose is an alignment tool that we will address in a deeper way in a later chapter, but for now, here is one of my purpose statements:

'I am all about the development and flourishing of others. I am about leaving each person better than I found them ... '

Speaking that to myself as one of the first thoughts of the day sets my focus towards the needs of those I lead and the opportunities presented to me to serve them, even in the heightened and strained action of the day in front of me. It offers a way to approach ordinary moments and imbue them with meaning and impact.

Find a phrase:

I am for ...

How am I?

How will I be experienced today? What will it feel like today to be on the other side of me?

'I will be gentle as well as brave today. I will be interested. I will be patient!'

How I am experienced is as important to me as what I accomplish. In fact, you can't truly divorce these things. Grab a feeling. Decide on one feeling you wish to be True of you today.

I want others to feel …

My Cave declarations for today:
  'I am creative and wise.'
  'I am for helping others become better'.
  'I want others to feel I am generous, thoughtful and kind.'
Your Cave declarations:

I am …

I'm for …

I will be …

These declarations, spoken, whispered or written in the Cave this morning, have the power to change the experiences, encounters and outcomes of today.

And tomorrow. Because, I'm training my brain to think this way, to look for this, to have a proclivity towards the True me, the Brave me, the Kind me and the Curious me.

SET YOUR MOOD

In 2005, the National Science Foundation[40] published research regarding human thought. They discovered that the average person has about 12,000 to 60,000 thoughts per day. I mentioned earlier that 95% of those are the same repetitive thoughts as the day before, but did you know around 80% are negative?

Rewiring your brain in the Cave is an attempt to rewire those repetitive tendencies and pursue a largely positive mindset. The Cave will help you set your mind. And it can also set your mood.

80% of our daily thinking is negative! Wow!

The mind is like Velcro for negative experiences and Teflon for positive ones.

RICK HANSON, POSITIVE NEUROPLASTICITY EXPERT[41]

What Hanson is saying is your adult mind has a bias towards 'no'. It has a tendency to register negative stimuli more readily than other stimuli, which means you have a high propensity to get into 'negative loop' thinking, about yourself and your life. It causes many of us to be risk adverse. And fearful.

According to psychologists, the negativity bias[42] was built into our brains to serve us in dealing with threats and to guard us against loss. The fight/flight/freeze mechanism of our brain saves us from danger and endows us with a natural tendency to place

---

40 The US National Science Foundation is an independent federal agency that supports science and engineering in all fifty states and US territories.
41 Rick Hanson PhD, *Hardwiring Happiness: The New Brain Science of Contentment, Calm, and Confidence* (Harmony, 2016), p36.
42 ibid., p35.

greater importance on potential negative outcomes than positive ones. 'No' becomes the dominant voice in our heads, and it acts like an autoimmune disease, shutting down possibilities.

Another view could be that the negativity bias is mostly learned. We have allowed the experiences of life to school us and then limit us, reducing much of our leadership to certain and cautious and sure. I'm sure that when I was younger, I tended to think more 'yes' than 'no' and it didn't always get me into trouble, in fact, it often opened up wonderful opportunities.

It is commonly accepted that people are either 'glass half full' or 'glass half empty' types and that these categories are part of our makeup, largely set. And yet the existence of RAS, and that system's dependence on human focus, tells me we have some agency here to set moods. If we can rewire our minds, we can also rewire our moods and set ourselves up for better.

The Cave is a place to set yourself for 'yes'. A setting of your mood to 'yes' is often accessed through gratitude. In fact, that might just be how you do it.

> Gratitude unlocks the fullness of life, it turns what we have into enough, and more. It turns denial into acceptance, chaos to order, confusion to clarity. It can turn a meal into a feast, a house into a home, a stranger into a friend.[43]
>
> MELODY BEATTIE

I have found, and so have many of my clients, that gratitude offers a helpful reframe to most experiences. If I can be grateful for what I do have, that which I don't have is put into perspective.

If my mind can land on and even lock into the positives rather than the negatives of each and every situation, it can set the mood for the day.

43 Melody Beattie, *The Language of Letting Go: Daily Meditations for Codependents* (Hazelden Publishing, 1990), p218.

'I get to' works way better than 'I've got to.'

I 'get to' … work – walk – meet – move – speak – travel …
I've 'got to' … work – walk – meet – move – speak – travel …

It's staggering to me how just changing one letter in a sentence can affect the entire way I show up at a day.

In the morning, I take a blank notebook into the Cave to write my 'I ams', but mostly to record my 'gratefuls'. I know it's a little mechanistic, but it changes things. When I set myself for gratitude, it shifts atmospheres.

I've seen this played out in a slum in Pune, India, as I worked with the Dalit people – those who have fallen out of the caste system; the lowest of the low, people who have nothing, often less than nothing, but have learned to reframe life in their favour.[44] And I've also seen it in executives who take responsibility to live above and beyond the fear they feel and choose to take time to celebrate what's going right and the people who've made those things happen.

They set their minds and direct their moods and fix characters and times.

Your Walk-on Tune

Often in the Cave, I also set my song. (Stay with me here.) Set your mood music.

My family is now grown and scattered, but we love to gather when we can and eat together. We will talk later in the book about the practice of the Table, but here it's helpful to let you know we often ask a Table question. One of our favourites is, 'What is your current walk-on tune?' I guess I'm assuming we are all celebrities or sports stars. For me, this is more than just a table game. I have a song in my head most days, that gets lodged there at the start of the day and has surprising power over the mood of my day. Maybe you do too?

---

44 'The Dalit: Born into a life of discrimination and stigma', *United Nations*, 19 April 2021, ohchr.org (accessed 14 August 2023).

For years, when the kids were growing up, if I didn't get ahead of the song, it became 'the wheels on the bus go round and round' or as they got older the lyrics to whatever boy band they were fawning over at the time. What I discovered was music affects moods. 'I'm walking on sunshine – ooooh ooooh' or 'I'm too sexy for my shirt' has a different vibe and puts a different lens on my day than 'Heaven knows I'm miserable now' or 'Hello darkness my old friend, I've come to talk with you again … '

Once again, you can set your song, as you set your mood and your mind. Is it 'Easy Like Sunday Morning'[45]? 'Eye of the Tiger'[46] 'Working 9 to 5'[47] Or 'Just Another Manic Monday'[48]?

Set your song, set your mood, set your day. Walk on.

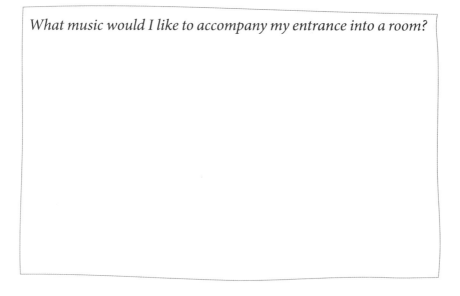

What music would I like to accompany my entrance into a room?

45 Lionel Richie, 'Easy Like Sunday Morning', Can't Slow Down, Motown, 1983.
46 Survivor, 'Eye of the Tiger', *Rocky III: The Eye of the Tiger*, soundtrack, Scotti Bros., 1982.
47 Dolly Parton, 'Working 9 to 5', *9 to 5: Original Motion Picture Soundtrack*, Columbia Records, 1980.
48 Susannah Carpenter and Vicki Peterson, 'Just Another Manic Monday', *Different Light*, Columbia Records, 1986.

Whatever you focus on this morning you give permission to exist today and will direct your life tomorrow.

The practice of the Cave is the quest of the True.

CHAPTER 4

TRUE:
in the Cave

To be what we are, and to become what we are capable of becoming, is the only end of life.[49]

ROBERT LOUIS STEVENSON

I was ashamed of myself when I realized that life was a costume party and I attended with my real face.

FRANZ KAFKA[50]

THE SUBTLE ART OF KNOWING

'Know thyself'

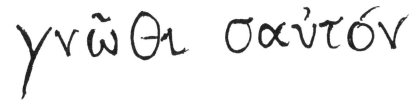

It's one of the best known of the Delphic maxims inscribed on the pronaos of the temple of Apollo at Delphi.[51] Attributed to just about every Greek philosopher, leader or playwright, it was later used by Socrates and Plato in their journey of self-discovery.[52]

49 Robert Louis Stevenson, *An Inland Voyage* (New York: Penguin Classics, 2001), p83.
50 This quotation is sometimes also attributed to Oscar Wilde.
51 Christopher Gill, *The Delphic Maxims: A Guide to Self-Knowledge and Self-Improvement* (Oxford: Oxford University Press, 2009), p1.
52 Plato, *Apology*, trans. G. M. A. Grube (Indianapolis: Hackett Publishing Company, 1975), 23a.

The leadership agency I founded is grounded in this same journey of self-awareness, self-discernment and self-responsibility. Why? Because you can't lead others (well) until you can lead yourself, and you won't lead yourself (well) until you get real with yourself.

Clients invariably come asking a number of action questions; questions designed to enable immediate impact:

How can I fix … ?
How can I grow … ?
Where can I bring about change in … ?
What shall I do about … ?

We will counter with a few deeper, foundational questions; know yourself questions like this:

What does it feel like to be the other side of you?
How are you experienced? By those close to you? By those you work with?
What are you for?
Why do you exist? What's the point of you?

These are culture, values, vision and purpose questions. At the core of this questioning, there's a True question, an identity question:

Who are you now?

All soul excavation begins with self-examination, facing the True you. The self that you must know is in this regard rather like an iceberg – what lies beneath is substantially more important for our quest than what sits on the surface. And what is below the water is significantly greater than what is initially seen - only 10% of the mass of an iceberg is visible above the ocean's surface.[53]

53 James S. Monroe and Reed Wicander, *The Changing Earth: Exploring Geology and Evolution,* (Brooks Cole, 2008), p253.

Encountering an iceberg can be perilously dangerous. You can never 'truly' or safely navigate one without reference to what remains under the water. To do so would be 'titanically' unwise.

As you seek to lead from a deeper place, it is these 'deeper places' that you must examine. To fail to do so risks the kind of dangers you encounter around icebergs. Think of the unpredictable leaders you've encountered in the past. You might navigate carefully around the perimeter on the surface, and suddenly you run aground on something completely uncharted. In the same way, what lies beneath your own leadership can cause shipwrecks among those you lead. And, ultimately, it can sink you.

Above the surface and below the surface is also happening in your brain. We have already discussed how our mind furnishes us with two types of thought, conscious thought and unconscious thought, and that our unconscious thought makes up around two-thirds of our current thinking. We can also picture this like an iceberg.[54]

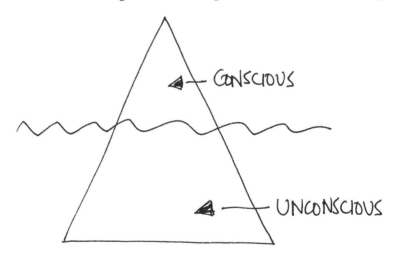

Getting to True is a deep work, significantly about making the unconscious conscious – bringing it to light and working out what to own and live from.

54 This is derived from the iceberg model of thinking, which is not attributed to any individual, although has been used by many to describe how much of our thinking is unconscious; Sigmund Freud is cited as an early user of this model.

I hope you are up for that. It might be messy and exposing work, it will probably not be an exercise you want to repeat, but if you do the dig, really do the work, you will find gold … at least, that is my experience.

WHAT LIES BENEATH

Until you make the unconscious conscious, it will direct your life and you will call it fate.[55]

CARL JUNG

Jung, described as one of the fathers of modern psychotherapy, pointed out what he saw in himself and others: people in positions of power who didn't know who they were, where they were going, or what it felt like to be the other side of them, underestimating the invidious impact they were having. We find ourselves in similar positions when we lead while wearing masks, hiding our True self from others and from ourselves. That which we are aware of, we often have choice about. That which we are unaware of has a habit of controlling us. Becoming aware of what lies beneath, of what is unconscious, is the gateway to healthy leadership.

Building on this concept, Jungian psychologist John Sanford saw the person as divided into 'idealised ego' and 'shadow,' or a pride position and a shame position.[56]

Sanford argues that we are happy to present and honour the aspects of our personality that bring us pride. And yet, much of what we are ashamed of, much of what makes up our 'shadow' side, much of what we try to mask, is also the very stuff of which our leadership is formed.

---

55 While this quotation does not appear in his published works, it has long been attributed to Carl Jung, likely from one of his lectures.
56 John Sanford, *The Kingdom Within: A Study of Jungian Psychology* (New York: Harper & Row, 1970), p123.

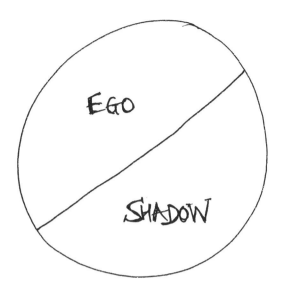

The fruit of our leadership is the overflow of our whole person, ego and shadow. Our hurts often make us, and our disappointments school us. Our failures form the ground of experience we refer to as we reach for future success. The things we once recoiled from, the things we thought would break us or undermine us, become the characteristics that define and make our leadership.

Every leader who desires to lead in this deeper way must face, acknowledge and know their own shadow side. If you don't know yourself, it's like walking in the dark. You keep bumping into things and falling over. You can't go anywhere very fast. It's limiting, painful and dangerous.

- *If you don't know yourself,* you will not take up opportunities for healing that will make your leadership healthier.
- *If you don't explore yourself,* you will miss out on being reconciled with your full and True self and then be unable to develop the very qualities and experiences that could really make you and fulfil you.

- *If you don't understand yourself,* you won't recognize the triggers that cause you to react in a certain way to certain people or situations. You will run the risk that, under pressure, the parts that are hidden will rise to the surface in an un-curated or uncontrolled way, one that will cause pain to yourself and others and will damage your work.

If you don't know yourself, you can't lead yourself, and you have little hope of leading others well.

77%

A recent survey carried out by media company UM, suggests that more than three-quarters of people in the UK (77%) suffer from Impostor Syndrome in some way.[57]

What if they discover that I don't know … ?
What if they realize I'm making this up as I go along?
When will they discover I'm actually a sham?

I have the privilege of coaching and consulting for some of the most incredible, successful and grounded leaders you could ever meet – business leaders, charity leaders, culture leaders. I have listened to the same question, often whispered, always haunting, sometimes explicit, often implied:

Have I really got what it takes?

I've asked the same question. More than once. If I let it linger, allow it to do its corrosive work, the answer comes back 'no.'

On one occasion, I found myself in the office of someone who was known by everyone as 'Coach.' For good reason. A revered and

---

57 Neil Franklin, 'Most people have no idea what imposter syndrome is, but they know they have it,' *Insight,* 18 December 2019, workplaceinsight.net (accessed 14 August 2023).

storied man who is honoured in two halls of fame, has won multiple Superbowls, and is known for his no-nonsense leadership skills.

I had been hired to help his team. My internal naysayer was doing overtime:

'You're trying to coach the coach?'
'Who the heck do you think you are?'
'You have no right!'
'What do you possibly have to teach him?'

The problem is invidious and deep. The imposter scripts that are well-rehearsed in us repeat undermining declarations that ultimately limit us. Until we force those scripts to align with truth. You see, the reason we fear and mask and justify has far less to do with the situation facing us and so much more to do with the backstory that formed us and our responses to it.

Recognizing this backstory and addressing the root cause, that which limits our beliefs and the way we behave, is not only very personal, it's also the first and most important step in a journey towards authenticity and integrity. Towards True.

Why do we feel shame and fear? Less than adequate? Why do we compare and compete? Why do we escape to comforts that ultimately don't bring comfort? Why do we perform to impress? Why do we strive to gain the approval that in the cold light of day we don't actually need? Why do we undermine the very things we desire most, in working to acquire the things that we will one day not care about? Why do we avoid being 'personally invested'? Why do we shut off emotion, numb our feelings and distance ourselves?

Don't be haunted by the question lurking in a darkened corner. Give it a seat at the Table – for a time. Hear it. Learn from it. Grow from it.

Answering these questions is to shine a light on the shadow side, dispelling its mystery. The more accurately we see ourselves, the less we need to wonder if we have what it takes, because we understand why we do. And where, in truth, perhaps we do not.

The answer is you very likely *do* have what it takes. What it takes is True, Brave, Kind and Curious. What it takes is you.

DO THE WORK

My coach won't work with me unless I'm 'doing the work,' and is challenging me to refine my thinking. My therapist is asking me really irritating questions that are, even more annoyingly, transforming me. And my spiritual director is praying with me and for me.

An executive coach, a therapist *and* a spiritual director? As a young leader I would have snorted at the thought!

But I've got issues. As have you. I've got influence. As have you.

And it's going to take some help to get there, a rummaging in the shadow, the scripts and the stories of our forming. Finding what is True is going to take honesty, humility and wisdom before it can have the impact it desires. I might need all the honest, humble and wise help I can get!

My therapist, Randy Powell, is a remarkable man, who has become a close friend. I'm not sure that it *should* work like that, but it really does! Randy also acts as part coach, thought partner and spiritual director to me. And that combination works wonderfully. Randy has thought, taught and written about truth, authenticity and integrity for years and much of my own work here I owe to our interactions. In one of our conversations, somewhere between talking about my brokenness, our bad golf games and how to help other leaders get healthy, he introduced me to his thinking around these attributes:

- *Honesty* is an approach to life and leadership that is not defensive and as transparent as possible. 'This is who I am!' Don't listen to the hype or believe the harsh critique. 'I'm a human being, having a go in a broken and beautiful world. I am the sum of my nature, my nurture and my choices. I'm committed to exposing the realities of my past and my limitations so that I might live in truth and strength in the present.'

- *Humility* is thinking about yourself correctly and acting accordingly. I used to teach that humility was not so much thinking less about yourself, as thinking about yourself less. But now I have come to see that humility is rather the ability to know your weaknesses and strengths and work on both as you live and lead in this world.

- *Wisdom* is a quality that all Soul Leaders possess. It is only found on the far side of honesty and humility, and it is rare. We lead in a world where information proliferates, knowledge is increasingly free, but wisdom is uncommon. Wisdom is found in the appropriation and application of that knowledge in real-life experience. It is knowing when to speak and when to be silent, when to give and when to receive, when to act and when not to. What to do and how. It is the honest, humble agency of choice.

Finding what is True is going to take being honest about yourself, humble in yourself and wise beyond yourself. This path is paved with tough conversations you need to have with yourself. You have to become *aware* of yourself. Then to *accept* yourself. Then you will need to *adapt* yourself. And finally, if you want to transform that which is around you, you have to *act* with boldness.

YOU CAN'T BUY SOUL OFF THE PEG

Santal 33 – Lagavulin 16 – Defender 90 – Pro V1 – ESV – Aesop Reverence – Shinola Linen Plain – Goodyear Welted – French cuff and links – BBQ meat – black tie events – wood-burner evenings

I.Y.K.Y.K.

We have, probably, all worked with colleagues who overdid the whole personality profile thing, who described themselves as a list of letters that others struggle to recognize. I have seen leaders who are burnt out as a result of operating in a style that is unnatural for them. More often I have been party to profiles being used to justify poor conduct, to excuse dysfunction or a lack of success.

> *'What would you expect from a Pioneer?'*
> *'They are a number 8; that's what 8s always do.'*
> *'I can't help it – I'm a feeler, it's just who I am.'*

So, one day, I got so sick of vanilla resumes, I made up my own simplistic preferences profiling system. Because really, sometimes the sorts of choices listed at the start of this section feel more revealing.

The truth is that none of this is truth!

While much of what is discussed, unpacked and revealed in the plethora of profile systems currently available offers insight into personal and relational conduct, this is not truth. It is all too easy to pigeonhole and reduce complex people into simplistic types. But labels are for products, not people. No system is nuanced enough to define you, nor must it limit you. These systems shouldn't box you or excuse you, be weaponised by you or anyone around you.

No algorithm or subsequent profile should be the end of the matter, only the start of a conversation. Let's continue that conversation. From the moment we become conscious of the world around us, our personality is being formed. Made up of our thoughts, feelings, influences, leanings and tendencies, it is the engine of our life and it is much bigger than a number or a series of four letters or descriptors that you can put underneath your signature on an email. There are, in reality, no helpful shortcuts on this journey. You can't develop character or really define your identity from a profiling system. You can learn a lot, and you will develop a vocabulary for understanding and tools for better conversations, but a profiling system will never define your soul.

Because your soul is unique.

As for me, I'm predisposed towards people over projects. I love flexibility over rigidity. The big picture is where I live and small detail is what I have to work on. I never know what I'm thinking until I start speaking. I tend to want to live in a future that I see as if it is already here. Significance is really important for me and making a difference can become too much of a driver. I find 'control' a toxin and those who try to control me I have to fight to not see as the enemy.

More pertinent still are pictures of the past. I am a seminal moment in the Royal Albert Hall at fifty. A 'yes' I said at twenty-four. Four births I witnessed in my twenties and thirties, an experience of loss at thirteen and multiple other seemingly innocuous experiences that meant the world to me. These things made me – they still make me. How I am to you is nuanced, layered and owes more to experience than DNA.

Same for you. All of this is the same for you, of you, about you.

If you wish to find what is True, you'll need a more holistic understanding. Maybe you want to use the space below to write down your unique combination? And the way in which you carry it.

Write your personality profiles down here:[58]

Write your tendencies down here:

Write your critical life moments here:

58 For example, Myers-Briggs, Enneagram, C-me Colours, 5 Voices, StrengthsFinder, etc.

Now write your enhanced, just for fun, anti-vanilla preferences profile:

By all means, if you have never done one, do a personality profile. Do two or more. Go deep to find out the superpowers of your type and the likely stress loops. Work out what is good for you and what is toxic. But remember this is just a starting point – the tip of the iceberg.

I have come to see myself as a smorgasbord made up of:

- *My Identity*: my personality, tendencies and preferences, which is impacted by my experiences and choices
- *My Ideologies*: the values and beliefs I espouse
- *My Injuries*: where I attempt to cover significant wounds
- *My Influences:* those I allow to be guiding voices in my life

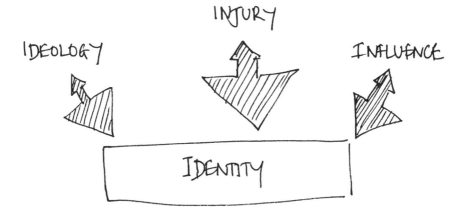

(And, if you're remotely interested, for me, all that translates into ENFP, NUMBER 3: with wing 2; Red / Yellow preference; Connector / Pioneer; Futuristic / Ideation / Communication / Woo / Empathy)

YOU ARE YOUR FORMING AS MUCH AS YOU ARE YOUR FORM

You are more than just your DNA; you are your experienced things, your received things, those learned things, those hurting things. You are also the healed things, the believed things and appropriated things. What results is unique. There is no one like you.

Sit with that.

As I write, the latest statistics estimate there are about 7.75 billion people living today, and the latest research suggests over 100 billion people have drawn breath on planet earth. And there is no one who shares precisely your combination of DNA, experience, preference and choices. 1 in 100 billion. That's rare.

Unique.

The staggering reality of utter uniqueness is also why comparison is so foolish and destructive.

COMPARE, COMPETE AND COPY

I'm sure that someone once told you that comparison is a thief; it robs you of joy and of time. What is truer is that comparison, when married to competition, is the real villain that does this. Comparison is itself just a part of socialization; we measure ourselves against others around us, which is a normal response, even a good one, one that will make us do better. A confident race is good.

Until it becomes an insecure fight.

The temptation for our races to become fights has never been more invidious. This generation is prone to compare their everyday existence on a swipe-by-swipe basis with several million other people's carefully photoshopped lives. It's a cultural deception which steals life and limits leadership. Influencers have never been more global. More baseless. The danger has never been more viral.

This is, of course, not an affliction reserved for teenagers. It becomes my poison when I allow my standards, my goals, ambitions, style and practice to be dictated to by another's. When I think that the way another CEO leads her staff is the way I should, when I allow other parents to set the standard for how I raise my kids, I risk renting someone else's way to be True, rather than owning my own. Comparison becomes my issue when I clock what my friends are driving, spending their money on, where they are holidaying and benchmark my life against this.

In truth, the brilliance that is in us, our ability to live into it and contribute to the world around us does not lie in how like everyone else we are, but rather, in how unique we really are and how we might utilize that difference for those we influence. How might we offer our uniqueness and bring different perspectives, other life experiences and greater value to the benefit of others?

IDEOLOGIES

Everyone loves a new device, anything that adds to the suite of other shiny things in the tech arsenal. And that new device comes with a default factory passcode that you are supposed to change to something personal, not guessable by anyone. The problem with default codes is they're not ours. The problem with default perspectives is they don't belong to us. Whether we are aware of them or not, those perspectives shape how we behave. These cultural values, religious beliefs and family norms that we've embraced might not be really ours. Some are beautiful and worthy – some are not. Some that have formed us really fit well and some just don't.

The quest of the True is a setting of a code, perhaps a new one.

Be slow to dismiss this as an exercise, for none of us are immune to default codes. We all carry 'unconscious bias'. There is no such thing as a blank sheet of paper; none of us turns up unbiased to a relationship or to a decision that has to be made. It's impossible to walk through this world and not process it through the lenses we've inherited and embraced.

> Without our permission or even awareness, stereotypes come to guide what we see, and in so doing, seem to validate themselves. That makes them stronger, more pervasive, and resistant to change.[59]
>
> JENNIFER L EBERHARDT

The real problem of 'unconscious bias' is the *unconscious* part. Pursuing what is True requires being conscious of the unconscious; lenses affect the way you see things, without you necessarily realizing. Your family will furnish you with a default, your experiences will clothe you with bias and your choices and their outcomes will affect your predispositions.

Becoming conscious is, in part, seeing the lens itself. And that means slowing down, interrogating yourself, asking the right questions, naming what you're truly believing and acknowledging what is shaping your life.

It is undoubtedly exposing and challenging to interrogate your past. Give yourself grace as you explore your heritage. Do it early. Do it before the generation who raised you pass on and all you have is their photos. Ask your questions while you can. Explore the 'Why?'s as well as the 'What?'s. Get curious about motives, drivers, expectations and dreams. Where does the thought that precedes

---

59 Jennifer L. Eberhardt, *Biased: Uncovering the Hidden Prejudice That Shapes What We See, Think, and Do* (Penguin Books, 2020), p10.

the action come from? What is the truth implicit in that thought? Is there a more fitting truth?

Consider what trends of your past could be active in your present. You must explore and debate, not as an act of rebellion, but as an act of honour.

We don't honour our forebears by embracing every one of their practices, but by choosing and consciously continuing some of their principles. There will be no honour unless we uncover and understand them. If we don't do this, we risk leading out of the overflow of principles we don't really ascribe to and acting in ways that are inconsistent with the very things that are important to us. Trespassing on somebody else's truth.

While potentially exposing, this exploration is the gateway to leading with the kind of passion and purpose reserved only for those who've wrestled their perspectives to the ground and written their own code.

More than this, you will need to be aware of how others have tried to intentionally shape our lives – and how that naturally includes a degree of them working out their own stuff, that might have nothing to do with us. While most people's plans for you will be well-meaning and not ill-intentioned, the path laid out for you by your school careers department, your favourite college professor, your life coach guru person or even by those who know you best will not always fit.

My father, who was my hero, once sat me down and told me he loved me and thought I was highly gifted. He told me I was inspirational as a speaker and leader. By this point, he had so filled up my approval bucket that I was ready to receive anything else he had for me. The next thing he said seemed innocuous at the time, but marked my life in a negative way for many years after:

'You are inspirational as a leader and a speaker, but you will never be wise. Just like me!'

He didn't mean to undermine or limit me with his myopic (and untrue) view of himself. But he did. For a time. Until I began to own my own perspectives. And realized, among other things, I am. I am wise. I carry wisdom, hard fought.

The things spoken over you do not need to be owned by you. Nor, for that matter, does the culture swirling around you.

While they may be transitory, societal trends have power to bend personal perspectives, and what is acceptable in 'this cultural moment' can tempt us towards convenient postures that are false, fake and just not you. Just not True.

Culture and tradition have more of an effect on reason and feelings than we often admit. The authorities that sway our leadership create a ready environment for some questions around authenticity. They can be approached in these terms:

Culture:
What do I truly stand for or champion?
What have I readily accepted or rejected that now sits uncomfortably with me?

Tradition – the way I was raised and brought up:
What do I never want to let go of?
What must I ditch if I am to have soul?
What did we celebrate? Speak badly of? Punish?

Reason:

Which beliefs that I hold, do I need to wrestle with lest they keep me bound to attitudes that are inherited and not truly appropriated?

What doubts do I have?

Feelings:

Which gut instincts and impulses, when brought into the light, really don't belong to me?

What have I borrowed from someone else that doesn't fit?

You don't need to accept it all, and you don't need to reject it all. But you may need to face it all.

See it – sift it – own it – believe it – live it – lead it[60]

Bring it all into the light. Break up with some concepts, double down on others and discover soul beyond self – within, because of and beyond yourself.

I know this is a difficult process, but you don't want to sleepwalk into your future holding onto a past that you didn't choose, or a present that doesn't fit, right?

- *Could your family deal with it* if you were to respectfully question some of their practices and reject some of their habits? Here's the thing: if you are to pursue True and lead fully from there, you must.
- *Could your community accept it* if you were to declare how you think differently and deeply about values, prejudices and principles? History tells us it will be difficult, but also that unprecedented health and growth can come from such a journey.
- *Could God handle it* if you were to express doubts over his nature, character or even existence to him? (Yes, of course, or he is not God, or not good.)

All I really know is you can never be True unless you think for yourself. And you will not experience healthy change unless you own it for yourself.

INJURIES

'Never trust a leader without a limp, but don't follow one with an open wound.'

60 Jennifer L. Eberhardt, 'How to Address Unconscious Bias' in *Stanford Social Innovation Review,* 2018.

If you read enough leadership books, before long, you'll stumble across the first part of this statement.[61] If you've been around life and leadership for long enough, the second half will also make sense to you. Leaders without limps have not been really tried, tested, and are only part grown. Trusting such a leader is risky, as you might have to go through their humbling experience with them. Following one who has not dealt with and allowed the wounds of their life to heal is a problem of different magnitude. Don't follow them; they will likely bleed all over you.

The process of healing is a 'fixing of character' that is vital for you and for everyone who follows you. Dealing with your wounds is required to lead from the soul, if it is to be a healthy soul that gives you that same quality of leadership as John or Jane.

HEALING THE WOUNDS

When you accidentally cut yourself, you clean and wrap the wound to stop bleeding and protect the damaged area from being impacted and reopened. That dressing must, however, be removed in good time, for it is only in the open air that protective scar tissue will form and enable the wound to heal properly.

What is true of wounds of the skin is also true of wounds that are deeper soul abrasions. They must be carefully opened up, in a safe environment, and allowed to heal. It's the only way to properly heal.

If you continue to cover up and protect those places where you carry an injury, you will not heal and you will not thrive. You will lead with an open wound. You might even bleed on those around you.

What I am discovering, however, is that with work, the wounds that I have protected can become the strengths I lead from. If I work through them, they can turn into an overcoming story, which can turn into empathy for others and strength. This is a process of intentional un-protection. You could say that exposure must precede closure, or you will never have it.

61 It is most often attributed to John Wimber, the Founder of the Vineyard Church movement.

How do we locate and open these protected places? The process is threefold. It involves paying attention to overreaction, becoming aware of projections and learning to acknowledge the games we play.

Overreactions

Have you ever noticed a slightly disproportionate reaction to certain people, to their conduct around you, to their treatment of you, or to the way they speak about you? Can you discern any instances where your responses seem out of kilter, unwarranted, exaggerated, or even 'catastrophized?' Are there regular patterns of self-sabotaging actions? Can you see a common thread, something that possibly triggers that response in you? What might the root be?

It may not be all that deep, or it could be life-crippling. It may not be your fault (you didn't choose it, it mostly happened to you), but it is your responsibility to deal with it and this awareness is an opportunity for healing.

Where are you wounded? How are you choosing healing?

Projection

Projection is a subconscious reaction. You see approaching you what you hate about you and find yourself judging them for it; the truth is you are judging you. If you've ever made an appointment to see a counsellor, likely this concept will have been discussed. It is seeing and judging what you deny and dislike in yourself as it comes towards you in the actions of another.[62]

I find it irrationally upsetting when someone is subtly manipulating me to do something I'm not sure I want to do because I hate the part of me that does that to others. The project is you. The projection is yours. What is it you hate coming towards you that you suspect might be a part of you? Becoming aware is half of the battle to heal.

---

62 Carl Jung has written about projection in numerous books, including *Psychology of the Unconscious (1912)*, *Two Essays on Analytical Psychology* (1928), and *The Archetypes and the Collective Unconscious* (Routledge, second edition 1968).

The Games We Play

We all play games. Games to protect ourselves, games to hide a weakness and games to assuage some fears. If we play the game well, we will get a pay-off from the game, but we will always pay a price. Some of us are good at hiding the games we play. But we all play games.

What we have to realize is that our short-term hit of whatever we were playing for comes at a long-term loss.

One of my clients is a large global service company. They approached me to work with their long-tenured executive team, who were struggling to lead the organization in a healthy way. I agreed a long-term project, with a distinctive rider written into the contract. The team had to take me out for dinner after each intervention and I got to choose the Table question.

One night, over a great meal and, if I remember rightly, a Sonoma Pinot, that question was:

'What psychological game do you play? What name do you give it? What do you get out of it? What impact do you think it has on your team and your leadership?'

It was a tense night. The seasoned and well-respected CEO began the process. There was resistance in the room, and in him. He looked at me and I thought it might be the last conversation we would have. Then, after a pause, he spoke. And slowly, carefully, he began to open up. He opened up about the games he used and why. In fact, he went way beyond the brief and spoke about things very personal to him. His game had a name and once it was named, it lost much of its nefarious power. One by one, others around the table followed suit, and when they didn't, their guardedness was noted and exposed.

That night broke some things well. The conversations were revealing, and the results have been healing. The team is undeniably different as an overflow of these nights. Be aware that most individuals play games, as do teams and organizations; you do too.

What games do you play?

I'm not asking you to stop them. Not yet. Just name them. Even that action will disarm the game. Call out the pay-off you get. Notice the price you pay. Even laugh about it. It will cease to be a game when you do.

'Healed people heal people and hurt people hurt people' is so well known you might even see it on a bumper sticker. Which doesn't make it any less true. It still remains that if you want to lead from your soul, you need to go after your healing. Aggressively.

Honour your limp, but deal with your wounds. You will carry your past, but you get to choose how – healed or hobbled, with open wounds or with scars.

INFLUENCES

You're the average of the five people you spend the most time with.[63]

JIM ROHN

Only five? Could it be possible that we are all the sum of *all* the people we give access to?

Everyone who speaks into our lives, influences us; it may be subtle or overt but we are giving permission for people to impact us with their input, example and opinion. Explicitly, implicitly and accidentally. We are of course more than the influences of the people around us, but we are not less.

I'm not suggesting you 'cull' your relationships (that feels aggressively brutal), rather that you learn how to filter the impact of those you do life with.

In *Good to Great*, Jim Collins emphasizes the importance of getting the right people on the bus.[64] This is like that! While he was

63 This quotation is often attributed to Jim Rohn, although it does not appear in any published work.
64 Jim Collins, *Good to Great: Why Some Companies Make the Leap – and Others Don't* (Harper Business, 2001), p41.

writing about an organization's staff, I mean your life's influences. You decide which voices are on the bus and heard at what volume. You need to work out the right seats, the right proximity to you, the right space for their ideas. This is about healthy, authentic friendship and healthy, authentic teamwork. It might also be about exiting some from the bus – those who don't need to be on the journey with you or are making the journey impossible.

Your bus should include perspectives unlike yours. You can't be authentic in an echo chamber. If everyone around you agrees with you, you'll end up thinking the same, speaking the same and acting the same. That's called leading a cult.

A Nigerian proverb asserts that 'it takes a village to raise a child'. In just the same way it takes a village to raise an authentic leader, so choose your people well.

THE PLAYERS IN YOUR CITY

'Have you considered that your relationships could do with editing? You might have given permission for the wrong people to have access to the most sacred spaces in your life.'

Remember my therapist/friend Randy? This was one of his many challenges to me, and he was right. As I processed my influences and laid out my relational network, he introduced me to his concept of walls and gates, and I have been using it and teaching it ever since. If you lend me your imagination, I can introduce it to you.

Your leadership life is like a medieval city with walls surrounding it and gates leading to interior spaces:

- The *walls* are thick to keep out enemies.
- The peripheral space just inside the walls is the *marketplace* – a bustling vibrant space for transactional dealings.
- The *courts* are inside the castle and are a safe place for close allies.

- But the *castle keep* – the strong rooms at the core of the defensive structure – is the personal, sacred space, kept only for those who hold your heart.

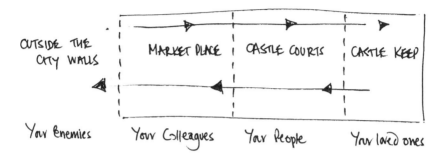

When you do your audit, filter from the inside out.

The castle keep

The keep is reserved for those who hold your heart. King Solomon, of gold mines and Queen of Sheba fame, was predominantly known for his wisdom and is quoted as saying, 'Above all else guard your heart, for it is the wellspring of life.'[65] The castle keep is a guarded place for the people you can be unguarded with.

The ancient Celts had a category of friendship that they called '*cymbrogi*.'[66] It meant: 'sword companions of the heart.'[67] The castle keep is for your *cymbrogi*; those who love you, fully; who will stand with you, permanently. My *cymbrogi* get me and let me be me. They have full permission to speak into me, and their voices are loud in my head and heart. I carry them with me. They carry me.

Leader, if you have friends who cannot hold your heart, they can't be in your castle keep. If you have friends who have defiled the sacred place, they need to be denied access, at least for a season. If you don't have *cymbrogi*, make it the quest of your life to find them and let them speak. It will save you.

65 Proverbs 4:23, *The Holy Bible* (New International Version).
66 John Koch, *The Celts: A History* (Wiley-Blackwell, 2009), p21.
67 'Cymbrogi' is more usually translated as 'comrades' or 'brothers in arms', meant to convey friendship that is stronger than blood relationships.

The castle courts

The courts are for the ones you do life with. At the risk of being too prescriptive, you will need three kinds of people:

- *Those you sit at the feet of:* These are your mentors. These people know more than you do, have known stuff for longer than you have, and generously share of their knowledge and experience with you. They need also to be your friends.
- *Those you look in the eye of:* These are your peers. They run, play, feast and dream with you. These people know you and support you. They are your friends.
- *Those you pour yourself into:* These are your apprentices. You might not call them this, but it's the relationship you have with them. You are intentionally pouring yourself into them. They are your friends.

These people need to know they are your people. Tell them. Often! Make space for their wisdom; it's coming from a good place.

The marketplace

This is your network. The relationships you build in the marketplace are contractual and transactional, not covenantal. I give and I get in return. Don't hear what I'm not saying – marketplace people can be your friends; they might grow to become your people, but they are your friends in a different way.

Don't mistake contracts for covenants. People who are in it, at least significantly, for what they can get out of it can be your friends, but they are so in a transactional way and cannot be given access to your heart, your fears or your dreams. Doing so is a risk that will inevitably lead to disappointment. Keep them in the marketplace until they can be trusted with the True you.

How do you tell who should get to go where? Unfortunately, human relationships are not an exact science. I have found two questions to be helpful:

1. Is there unhealthy competition in the relationship?
True friends don't compete. They might play golf together and try to win, they'll engage in friendly competition, but they don't really compete in life. Wherever one is trying to get ahead of another in the things that are truly important, that relationship is most likely transactional. It can be really beneficial and healthy, but it is not safe in the way that your castle keep people are safe. If your 'friend' always has a better story, a worse pain or needs the moment to be about them, they are not *cymbrogi*. If their practice is to consistently hijack your thing, and they need to always come out on top, they do not get to be in the most vulnerable places.

2. Is there attempt to control the relationship?
True friends don't need friendship on their own terms. True friends don't need me to be who they need me to be in order for me to be their friend.

The city walls
The city walls and gates provide exit and entry and are designed to keep enemies out. Use them well. From the Latin root of the word enemy, *inimicus* literally means 'not a friend'. Working out who are 'not your friends' will save you from much pain, loss, and anxiety. An ancient Arab proverb claims, 'It is better to have a thousand enemies outside the tent than one inside the tent.' Heed this well and process it often.

We might think of enemies as easily spottable Bond villains, but they can be the everyday people working against you; they're in opposition to your authentic life and you should be very wary when dealing with them in the marketplace.

I want you to think about two things as far as permissions are concerned: access and volume. Who goes where? How loud is their voice? Do an audit. And let people go. Not in a confrontational or literal manner, but through changing their proximity to your heart and by turning down the volume of their voices. Also call people in. Bring closer those who edify your life and help you be a truer you and a better you.

To be True, you must get to the core of you – your DNA, your experiences and what you believe. While this is in many ways an independent exercise, it can never be fully so – your connections become you. The people you permit to influence the True you will become part of you. Health here will result in health out there.

HIHO.

Finding what is True and being True to who you really are is the starting point for leading with soul.

If a leader can't find themselves, they are not only lost, but everyone who follows will also be lost. If they can't keep the promises they make to themselves, they can't really, with integrity, commit to others in leading them. So pause. This is a moment to covenant with yourself for the sake of your soul.

> I will dig. I will seek to be aware – of who I am and why that is so, of how I show up and where it came from. I will look to question and reflect on the perspectives I have inherited and the truths I have believed, to devote myself to some, to reject others out of hand, and to hold lightly to dogmas I previously stood my life on. They might not take my weight.
>
> I will work to heal, no longer to cover up or hide my wounds, but give them air and treatment so they might become the sort of scars that tell of lives well lived and skirmishes come through.
>
> I will take responsibility for the influences I allow. I will filter with gentleness, but curate with strength those I will allow around my table and in my ear, to have my back and carry my heart and inspire my leadership life. This is on me.[68]

BRENÉ BROWN

To be True.

---

68 Brené Brown, *The Gifts of Imperfection: Let Go of Who You Think You Should Be and Embrace Who You Are* (Avery, 2010), pp106–107.

THE CAVE

THE TABLE

THE FIRE

THE ROAD

CHAPTER 5

THE ROAD:
the way of the Brave

A spring morning in the middle of the 1960s, a man in his fifties placed into his homemade wooden wheelbarrow a pick, an axe, a shovel and a lunchbox. He trundled his cargo south from his crofthouse door down a familiar narrow rutted bridlepath, up and down Hebridean hillsides, along the hazardous cliff faces, through patches of bent and stunted hazel and birch over quaking peat bogs.

After almost two miles he stopped and turned to face homewards. Before him and to his left were steep banks of bracken, turf, birch and hazel. To his right, green pastureland rolled down to the sea. There were sheep on this pasture and, close to the shore, a small group of waist-high stone rectangles which once, a century ago, had been the thatched cottages of a community called Castle. The vestigial masonry of a medieval keep teetered on an outstanding crag a few yards from the deserted homesteads, melding into the bedrock so naturally that, 500 years after they were first erected and 300 years since they were last occupied, it had become difficult to tell from a hundred yards away where the remnant walls of the man-made fortress finished and the natural stone began.

Then, alone in an empty landscape, he began to build a road.

He started by widening his workspace. He cleared the scattered clumps of wind-blasted native woodland which lay on either side of the old track. He chopped the dwarf trees down, and he dug up their roots. He gathered the detritus carefully into piles at the edge of his planned route. He worked a long day. He was accustomed to working long days.

At the end of the first long day, when he reassembled his equipment in the wheelbarrow and began his walk home, he had denuded several yards of ground. He had, in fact, accomplished slightly more than one-thousandth of a task which would take him twenty years to complete, which would pay him not a material penny and would cost him little more, but which would leave his manifesto marked in stone upon his people's land.

His name was Calum Macleod. He belonged to the township of South Arnish in the north island of Raasay.[69]

CALUM'S ROAD BY ROGER HUTCHISON

To say that roads are important is to state the completely and utterly obvious. For the Romans, their famously straight roads were the formation and foundation of the empire, the means of moving soldiers and supplies, and conquering, subjugating and settling the local population. For the ancient Chinese, Persian and Greek traders the Silk Road, the network of trade routes linking China and the west over land and sea, was the means of exchange of ideas and goods. And crossing much of Europe are vital arteries: a latticework of old drover's roads, salt paths and pilgrims' ways, now often overlaid by motorway networks.

For North Raasay, a road meant a way for children to get to school, a way for groceries to be delivered, a way to get to the hospital or the ferry. A way to save an island community from dying. And Calum's road, which took him nearly twenty years to build, has become something of a legend.

The road that takes me home from the highway to my driveway is not unlike Calum's. Half a mile of single track, stony and potholed, shadowed with ancient pines, the beech-hedge-lined route is special to me because of what it promises at the end of it. It's the way in, the way home.

But more important perhaps, my road is the way out, the route

69 Roger Hutchison, *Calum's Road: The Story of a Man Who Built a Road to the End of the World* (Canongate Books, 2002), p10.

to adventure. In the early morning, mist clearing over the glade of trees across the valley, the tires crunch the gravel as I pull away from the still-sleeping household, and the engine grinds up the craggy, rutted hill. That hill, so familiar, looks different every day – ice bound and dangerous in the dark of winter, flecked with sharp low light in the dawn of summer. As I steer around potholes and slap through puddles, I've learned to keep alert to rabbits and hares, startled roe deer or stupid pheasants, as I set out into purpose and possibility. Every trip to see a client begins on this road, every flight to a company headquarters or to a team offsite, to a teaching or an intervention, starts here, on this road. And it is a metaphor for what I do. Each day, the thing that I set out on, whether that is from my leather study chair or a hotel room on the other side of the world, the thing that enables me to connect and communicate with others, to contribute and add value, to make a difference and leave a legacy, is my *Road*. For me, currently, that takes the shape of Arable, the leadership consulting business I founded.

For Calum, his Road was literally building a road. His purpose, his 'why', his dream, what he was for, was regenerating his island home community. The way he did it was by building a road. At the age of fifty-two, having encountered decades of excuses and postponements from the Inverness council, he came to the decision to build the road himself. It took a pickaxe, a shovel, a wheelbarrow and years of backbreaking hard labour, and it took on the shape of a calling, a vocation, a protest. And that is what he came to be remembered for. He was a lighthouse keeper, a crofter, a husband and friend. But those things are not what he is remembered for. Calum's road was his Road.

A Road is connection; a Road is work; a Road is a means to an end. And day after day after day you have to put your pickaxe and your shovel in a wheelbarrow and set out on it.

What is your Road?

If your Cave is about being True, finding yourself and leading soulfully, your Road is then about living bravely, finding your reason for being and working out how to live it. You may be for great leadership, so perhaps your Road is coaching leaders in a leadership coaching consultancy. You may be for truth and the value of people's stories, so perhaps your Road is building a publishing house. You may be for making things faster, better, beautiful, ending poverty, making people well, seeking justice. Your Road may be your work in a tech company, a beauty salon, a hospital trust, an aid agency or it may be something quite different.

A Road is what can get you from where you are to where you need to be. It is how you change things. Whatever it looks like, there's a Road that you must choose, and you must set out on it, every day, and stay on it, in the midst of the kind of distractions and the type of speedbumps, roadblocks and dead-end avenues that beset all leadership lives.

So pick a Road.

Because it all starts with picking. Exercising the power to choose is to be Brave in its rawest form. For Calum, the decision to refuse powerlessness or passivity was Brave. He chose to act; he then chose his Road. It is just the same for you and for me.

Victor Frankl, Holocaust survivor and eminent psychologist, is often quoted as saying:

> *Between the stimulus and response, there is a space. And in that space lies our freedom and power to choose our responses. In our response lies our growth and our freedom.*[70]

70 Stephen R. Covey, *The 7 Habits of Highly Effective People: Powerful Lessons in Personal Change*, Rev. ed. (Free Press, 2004), p94.

Frankl's story of incarceration, torture and loss inspired his life's work in human nature. He comments on his experience of having everything taken from him except this choice:

The last of the human freedoms – to choose one's attitude in any given set of circumstances, to choose one's own way.[71]

The Brave choice for you is also firstly to choose. Deciding against a shoulder-shrugging acquiescence or worse, a victimhood, and choosing to choose Brave instead. Choosing to be True and then choosing to bring your influence and agency to bear. Your Road starts here; you must choose to walk a Road. And which Road?

WHAT3WORDS? OR CHOOSING THE RIGHT ROAD

If a man does not know to which port he sails, no wind is favorable.[72]

SENECA THE YOUNGER

In 2013, four guys were trying to solve a problem they had with a music events company that was struggling to deliver equipment and people to remote locations.

They came up with a system that divided the entire world into 3m squares and applied a three-word code to any and every square. And it became the geocode business What3Words. It acts like a trig point or a fixing location so you can find where you're going anywhere on the planet. If you want to send a bouquet of flowers to the residence of the Prime Minister of the UK, the front door at 10 Downing Street, London is: ///SLURS.THIS.SHARK. If I want to meet you at the statue of Thierry Henry outside Arsenal's football stadium in north London, it would be: ///UNITS.REMIND.GAVE.

71 Viktor E. Frankl, *Man's Search for Meaning.* 4th ed. (Beacon Press, 1992), p86.
72 This quotation is most often attributed to Roman Stoic philosopher, Seneca the Younger. It was quoted in *The 7 Habits of Highly Effective People* by Stephen R. Covey, who says he found it in an unspecified library book.

(See you there on match day!) Weird and yet decidedly simpler and stickier than the GPS coordinates it was designed to replace. Which would be 51° 33' 17.5212' N / 0° 6' 32.8032' W. Less complex and yet more specific.

When I'm coaching a client or a team into their preferred future, I'm looking to use a similar code. Three words:

///MOVE.FIT.FILL

Less complex than most coaching questions, but perhaps more specific and hopefully stickier! It might not locate you, but it will lead you into your purpose and help you work out how to fulfill it.

What *moves* you?
What *fits* you?
What *fills* you?

- *What moves you?* What is your biggest dream? What gets you up in the morning? Or keeps you awake at night? What would you love to contribute, change, fix, speak into … ?

  We started this conversation in our Cave chapters, but now in a more granular way, I want you to think about what motivates you. Understand this: what moves you will make the Road meaningful for you and those you lead.

- *What fits you?* What is your strongest gift to the world? What do you do better than almost anyone you know? Be precise, not ambiguous or general. What is it? How is it? Why is it special?

  What fits you will make the Road useful to you and the people you work with.

- *What fills you?* What is your deepest joy? What lights you up? What activities or experiences bring great fulfilment? What fills you will make the Road sustainable for you and your leadership.

Somewhere in the centring of these three questions lies a purpose. And importantly, a way to achieve it. As you ask these questions, resist the temptation to belittle or apologise for the process or your answers. This is your life, not a dress rehearsal of it. Stop waiting in the wings for someone to give you a cue, hanging back until the perfect moment to play for real. This is it! Resist timidity; no one prospers from you playing small.

What these questions are drawing you into is not a self-indulgent adventure. Your responses should disrupt your thinking so you might lead other people, with disruptive care, into a better reality.

This process might just amount to a recalibration towards an activity that suits you better, or in a grander way, it might spur you to step fully into your life's contribution, your destiny or what Nietzsche called your 'life's task'.[73] I don't know which it will be for you. But what I do know is every attempt to lead from a deeper place is a revolt against a system that encourages conformity, wants us to stay in our lane, and thereby constricts the soul.

Move

Without a dream, purpose withers; without wonder, hope stagnates. What is your dream? It's probably accessed through a complaint, or the places we see a lack or gap. Ask yourself:

73 Friedrich Nietzsche wrote about finding one's 'life's task' and coined the term *Ubermensch*, which was his idea of how humans could evolve to a higher state of being, if willing to challenge oneself and overcome weakness.

What is missing?

*What is it that really bothers me? About life? Society?
My current context?*

What would I love to be able to fix, solve or address?

What would it look like if … ?

What might be created if … ?

*What might there be, that is not there now, if I step into my
dream?*

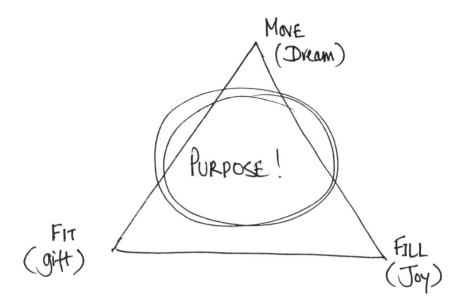

MOVE (Dream)

PURPOSE!

FIT (gift)

FILL (Joy)

Fit

The question of 'fit' is more about acknowledging your gifts. One spring morning I had been called in to help a private equity firm support their latest acquisition in managing some relational challenges in their team. As we talked, I listened to a raging debate between seasoned executives, as they tried to work out what they were each good at. Most of them had fallen into their current roles or been promoted because they were good at something they now no longer did. Others had never known or been able to articulate what their unique contribution was.

I gave them these three words and asked that they start with fit. What fits you? As they began to recognize and honour the unique giftings and real contributions around the table the groundwork was being laid for what has become a seriously healthier executive team.

You might want to do the same.

Could you consider doing an informal 360-degree review? Not the kind of review that's rooting for weakness, but rather one that celebrates strength? Remember our definition of humility? Thinking correctly about yourself. Ask some friends, those who have your back, the following questions. Then answer them for yourself. Write them down.

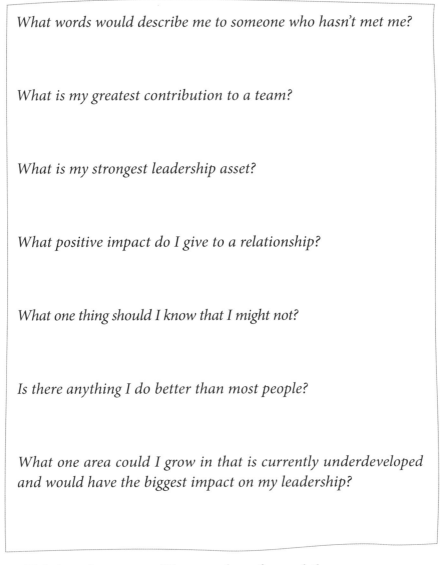

What words would describe me to someone who hasn't met me?

What is my greatest contribution to a team?

What is my strongest leadership asset?

What positive impact do I give to a relationship?

What one thing should I know that I might not?

Is there anything I do better than most people?

What one area could I grow in that is currently underdeveloped and would have the biggest impact on my leadership?

This is so important. Hang out here for a while.

In our current cultural moment, we are so keen to inspire the next generation to 'run with their dreams'. It's a great admonition. But not more important than finding something you do better than a thousand other people. Alignment in passion *and* skill is critical. It's the combination that will lead you into purpose.

Fill

Name what gives you joy. Joy is often overlooked as an indicator for purpose, but if you are going to persistently and sustainably lead from your soul, you will need to discover and apply whatever your soul loves. Nietzsche advocated that 'the way to discover what you were put on this earth for is to delve back into your past experiences and list the times that you felt most fulfilled and see if you can draw a line through those events and moments.'[74] What links them?

Human beings are drawn to the places, people and activities that fill our hearts with joy. Of course they are – you don't need science to tell you that. Human beings also stick at and pursue the places, people and activities that bring them life.

Here's the science anyway: Angela Duckworth, author of *Grit: The Power of Passion and Perseverance*,[75] contends that those who do what they love are exceedingly more likely to stick with it. She developed a Grit Scale for West Point, the US Military Academy, measuring both passion and perseverance around various activities and found there's a correlation between the two, and the result is grit. What she calls 'passion' is not a fleeting interest, but something with an enduring magnetism to our soul – that which fires us up, time and time again.

There have been hundreds of studies done across every profession under the sun, and the aggregated data indicates people

74 Friedrich Nietzsche, 'Schopenhauer as Educator' in *Untimely Meditations* (Trans. R. J. Hollingdale, Cambridge University Press, 1983), pp85–168.
75 Angela Duckworth, *Grit: The Power of Passion and Perseverance* (Scribner, 2016), pp107–108.

are (perhaps too obviously) more satisfied and perform at higher levels in their jobs and are happier in their life overall when they experience consistent joy in what they're doing.[76] Joy is not insignificant in our success.

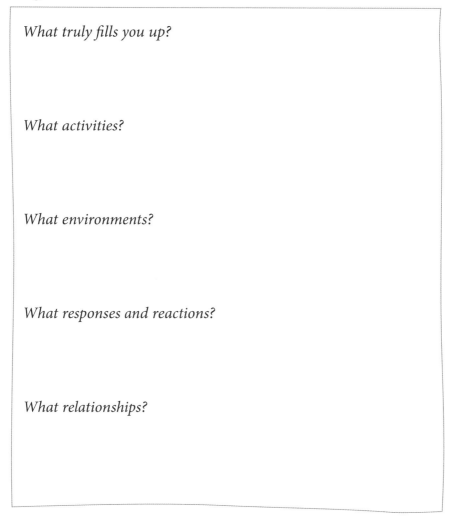

What truly fills you up?

What activities?

What environments?

What responses and reactions?

What relationships?

76 Studies have found a link between passion and productivity – passionate employees are more engaged, more creative and innovative, more willing to give effort and go the extra mile for clients, and even have better physical and mental health. Such studies come from the Gallup Organization, the Harvard Business Review, University of Pennsylvania, the Society for Human Resource Management, and the journal *Psychological Science*.

Consider your dreams, gifts, and joys. Spend time in them, with them. While it may feel superficial and self-indulgent, this exercise in intentionally showing up most effectively for the people around you at the task before you is quite self-less. When you engage with your 'unique contribution,' you will find you bring your best. You create an environment where it's possible and optimal for others to do so as well, and everyone wins.

What is your current purpose statement? This is a statement of intent: 'this is what I am for, this is what I'm going after.' This is your YES.

Remember, we are looking for an area, not an exact point, and understand this is not fixed in perpetuity. You can grow and flex according to context, season and necessity. This area is dynamic and can change over time. What I was passionate about when I was twenty I wouldn't express in the same way now that I'm fifty, and who knows exactly what I will be doing when I'm seventy.

What NOW moves you?
What NOW fits you?
What NOW fills you?

So pick a Road. And start walking.

WHAT ARE YOU CARRYING?

*We must be willing to let go of the life we planned so as to have
the life that is waiting for us.*[77]

JOSEPH CAMPBELL

Deciding to act purposefully begins by deciding to not act in
conflict with your purpose. The very word 'decide,' comes from the
Latin combination of two words: *off* and *cut*.[78] To cut off. To make a
purposeful choice, you must first let go of other choices.

If choosing your purpose is about finding and living your yes,
focus is about 'defending that "yes" with a thousand "no"s.'[79] No to
anything that is not you, not currently you. No to anything that
is not YES. You must say no to lesser yeses, other people's yeses,
yesterday's yeses, counterfeit yeses.

No is an invitation to stop carrying responsibilities, roles and
tasks that are weighing your purpose down. How much of what
holds you back, limits your effectiveness and weighs you down, is
not actually yours to carry? You just shoulder it anyway.

Consider four bags. Four bags that most people and most
organizations carry: your bag, somebody else's bag, nobody's bag
and God's bag.[80]

77 While this quotation is not in a publication, it is often attributed to Joseph Campbell,
and he addresses very similar ideas in his book, *The Hero with a Thousand Faces*.
78 William Morris, *Etymological Dictionary of the English Language* (Dover
Publications, 1968) p134.
79 Jeff Walker, *Launch: How to Jumpstart Your Business, Build a Tribe of
Customers, and Take Control of Your Life* (Morgan James Publishing, 2015), p146.
80 The four bags concept is thought to have been developed in the 1980s and
1990s, and is sometimes attributed to Jim Rohn.

- *Your bag:* This is the bag you must carry. It's your entrustments. It's what has been given to you by virtue of who you are, and how you are best designed to show up in this world. It's your identity and your purpose. This bag is the activity surrounding your unique contribution to this world. You were made for this! Grab this bag tightly!

- *Somebody else's bag:* This is the bag of the greatest opposition to your purpose, because you carry it so well. You are excellent at most of the activities connected to this bag. You may have heard it said that good is the enemy of great? Yes? Think of it this way: general excellence is the enemy of unique and extraordinary.

  Somebody else's bag is the enemy of your bag. Attraction to this bag is especially strong for those who have labelled themselves 'a good allrounder' or more negatively 'Jack of all trades, master of none.'

  The leaders I coach who tell me they are allrounders often find they've been carrying somebody else's bag for most of their careers. This bag is the bag you pick up because no one else has. It's your duty bag; ironically, it thwarts you in doing your duty – leading with *your* purpose. It thwarts the rightful owner of the bag, too, by standing in the way of what's theirs to take on.

  Pass the bag on.

- *Nobody's bag:* This is the bag we inherited, passed on to us. There was a time when carrying this bag was important, it is not now, and yet 'nobody's bag' is carried by plenty of leaders. We tend to collect more responsibility than anyone can carry well. Seldom, however, do we allow ourselves to let go of good things. Organizations are particularly bad at carrying nobody's bag, and yet, doing so dilutes effort, limits productivity and undermines performance.

  Cancel the bag!

- *God's bag:* This bag is heavy. Of course it is, it's designed to be carried by a superpower. Whether you believe in God or not, this bag is weighty.

  This is the bag of all the emotions and responsibilities you feel for all the stuff you can't ultimately control. In my experience, this bag is the hardest to let go of. You will likely wrestle with this all your life. But wrestle with this you should, and let it go you must, for if you don't, its weight will overwhelm you.

  Let go of the bag.

Take an inventory of your bags

Ask yourself how much time and energy you give to each bag. Take two weeks of your schedule and do a forensic analysis. Your activity will consist of things that pertain to:

1. Your yes – your unique offering
2. Your excellence – things you are really good at
3. Your competence – things you can do
4. Your incompetence – things you're really bad at

Track how much time you spend on each.

The enemy of your 1 is not your 4 – it's your 2 or 3. Retain some of your 4 – it keeps you humble and human. Attempt some DIY when you are not very good at it; paint a wall when you could get someone much better, far quicker and significantly tidier. But maximise 1. Make space for your yes. Fight against the tendency to live in 2 and 3.

Spring clean the closet of your leadership in the same way you clear out your wardrobe once a year and take things to the charity shop or pass them on to someone else. In the same way you clean your shed and throw away old things and hide the tools you didn't tell your partner you bought!

Pass some bags on. Do it carefully, over time, but let them go. Delegate the things you do passably to those who will do them excellently and then let them go. Have some good cremations of some bags that should have been laid to rest many years ago. Do it respectfully, but do it. Remember, we don't honour our forefathers by embracing all their practices, but rather by consciously living by some of their principles. Let the bags go.

Give God, or the universe or fate or whatever you think it is, their big bag back. Do not take responsibility for the things you have no control over. Make a list of the things that you feel responsible for, even anxious about. Now delete anything from the list that you have little or no material control over. Even that small step is a revolt against overcarrying.

Pause here again.

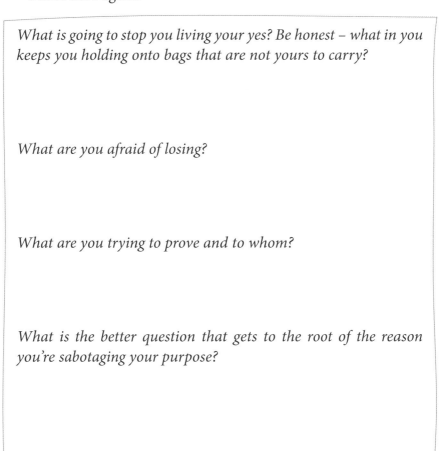

What is going to stop you living your yes? Be honest – what in you keeps you holding onto bags that are not yours to carry?

What are you afraid of losing?

What are you trying to prove and to whom?

What is the better question that gets to the root of the reason you're sabotaging your purpose?

Now, double down. If the Road is chosen with purpose and walked with focus it is only completed with resilience.

KEEP MOVING FORWARD

So pick a Road, pick up your bag and start walking. Now. Move. Thinking about it is thinking about it – doing it is doing it!

Free yourself from the lie that there is a perfect answer. There are better answers and maybe a best answer, but a perfect choice does not exist. Decide for one direction, for one person, for one option. Make it specific. Make it accountable. Do it now.

Don't let the fear of getting it wrong rob you of the bravery of having a go. Dethrone 'perfect' by understanding it to be the enemy of progress. Don't wait for your perfect moment; that moment is most likely found as you stumble through the many imperfect moments on your Road.

A well-known advertising agency I've been working with has recently adopted the phrase and policy 'roughly ready' as a way to counteract the culture of perfectionism that was suffocating creativity and progress. How about you also adopt 'roughly right'? I've personally observed that the final 15% of any project I'm working on takes about 75% of the effort of the entire undertaking and adds about 1% of value to the finished product. I know that I have no science to back this up, but it doesn't make it any less real.

MAKE AGGRESSIVE MISTAKES

One of my leadership heroes is Brian. Brian is a whiskey-drinking, bike-riding, adventure junkie and my friend. He is one of the kindest, most grounded and most inspirational leaders I know. His organization is currently right at the heart of healing divides over race in their city; they support work in the slums of India and the townships in South Africa. Brian's team runs an incubator for entrepreneurs and a garage to receive donations of used cars, so they can fix them up and give them as gifts to those who need transport but can't afford it. Brian is a larger-than-life leader of the largest church I know, with franchises all over the US. Over 35,000 people show up across his city to experience and participate in what I can only describe as 'church of a different kind.'

Brian is well known for encouraging his leaders to make aggressive mistakes, not passive ones, and giving them space to try. Even as I write this down, it feels like too much. Aggressive mistakes?!

His point is twofold:

1. You will make mistakes. So, stop trying not to make mistakes. It's impossible, and consequently, a pitiful practice. Just decide to make front foot mistakes, rather than back foot ones, offence mistakes as opposed to defence mistakes. Better to be found lacking 'having a go' than caught out hiding.
2. Passivity is detrimental to everything meaningful in your life.

Everything. Take that in.

Keep moving forward. Show up for life, don't just let it show up *at* you. Doing so *will* propel you into risk. Don't hide from it, run from it or deny it; own it.

Reframe your thinking around failure. Depersonalize it by seeing it and speaking of it as an event not an individual. See it as learning. If you believe failure to be final, you will live risk-averse and become adventure-less.

With your purpose in your mind's eye, get moving, and then keep on moving. Moving might be learning, by apprenticing yourself to someone better than you or pitching your idea repeatedly until it becomes clearer and more compelling. It could be making product and then iterating on that product and selling it door to door. Moving might be taking a class at night school or quitting a job that you know is wrong.

But pick a Road. Pick up your bag. And start walking. Do it now.

The practice of the Road is the way of the Brave.

CHAPTER 6

BRAVE:
on the Road

The bravest are surely those who have the clearest vision of what is before them, glory and danger alike, and yet notwithstanding, go out to meet it.[81]

THUCYDIDES

I learnt that courage was not the absence of fear, but the triumph over it. The brave man is not he who does not feel afraid. But he who conquers that fear.[82]

NELSON MANDELA

On 11 February 1990, after twenty-seven years of incarceration for fighting his country's discriminatory Apartheid system, Nelson Mandela was released from prison. Four years later, he became the President of South Africa. His story is a masterclass in the kind of leadership we are talking about – we could have used it to illustrate each and every one of our soul qualities.

He spent the first eighteen years of his time at Robben Island Prison confined to a cell 2m x 2.5m with only a rough folded blanket on a concrete floor for a bed and a bucket for a bathroom. He was given half an hour in the exercise yard each day. He was allowed to write and receive one letter every six weeks. And he was allotted one visitor for half an hour once a year. In that personal Cave he set himself for what he describes as 'the most difficult task in life … changing yourself.'

81 Often attributed to Thucydides, Greek historian, who died in 400 BC.
82 Nelson Mandela, *Notes to the Future: Words of Wisdom* (Little, Brown and Company, 2013), p123.

He was Kind: he taught other prisoners not to retaliate when they were badly treated. He won over all of the guards and later this was remarkably demonstrated in the Tables he hosted, which were made up of enemies as well as friends, both who became allies. Trust built, and covenants hard won.

He was Curious, and formed an education programme in the limestone quarry where the prisoners broke rocks each day, encouraging each one to teach whatever they knew whenever they were able. This became known as the 'Robben Island University'. He studied his captors and what motivated them. His particular combination of radical openness and unapologetic forgiveness led to the forging of a future for his people and a new shape for the nation.

It is, however, a resolute bravery that marked and made his leadership journey. He was, above all, Brave. The Road he chose was the Road to freedom; he approached it with a clarity of purpose, a forensic focus and an obdurate resilience in the midst of opposition. This is what it's going to take to bring your quest for your True to your context in a healthy way. It's the way of the Brave.

Five years before he was finally released, in the wake of growing international pressure, the incumbent, President PW Botha, offered Mandela his freedom on the understanding that he would retire his agenda and renounce conflict. At a rally in Soweto, Mandela refused Botha's demands in the form of a letter read by his daughter Zizi:

I cherish my own freedom dearly, but I care even more for your freedom. Too many have died since I went to prison. Too many have suffered for the love of freedom. I owe it to their widows, to their orphans, to their mothers, and to their fathers who have grieved and wept for them.

Not only I have suffered during these long, lonely, wasted years. I am not less life-loving than you are. But I cannot sell my birthright, nor am I prepared to sell the birthright of the people to be free. I am in prison as the representative of the people and of your organization, the African National Congress, which was banned.

What freedom am I being offered while the organization of the people remains banned? What freedom am I being offered when I may be arrested on a pass offence? What freedom am I being offered to live my life as a family with my dear wife who remains in banishment in Brandfort?

What freedom am I being offered when I must ask for permission to live in an urban area? What freedom am I being offered when I need a stamp in my pass to seek work? What freedom am I being offered when my very South African citizenship is not respected?

Five years later, Mandela was finally released; nine years on, his courageous stance enabled him to lead his nation to a new kind of freedom.

Being resolutely Brave changes things. That's what leadership is supposed to do, right?

It is a Brave soul who nails ninety-five propositions to a German door, that chains itself to a parliamentary railing, that sets sail to a new world in the hope of freedom. It's a Brave soul who refuses to take the destruction of our planet lying down, and actively searches for real solutions. The Brave soul has a dream, speaks it and walks it out whatever the circumstances.

I don't know what being Brave looks like for you. What I do know is you will accomplish little without it. Those declarations and resolutions you make in the Cave need a Road for them to become a reality. That Road is rarely easy, it is usually long and often rocky, there may be a stone in your shoe, the sun will beat down, the wind will blow in your face and it will rain. In this regard the Road doesn't foster or pander to passivity, it will draw you out and disturb you. Those who would walk it will inevitably meet with resistance. Resistance from comfort. From expedience. From compromise. Resistance that counsels: 'Keep your head down', 'Stay in your lane', 'Don't rock the boat', 'Settle for what you have'. But if you as a leader want to change anything, if you are aiming for a fixing – in you and in the culture around you – there is only one way to bring it about: the way of the Brave. It's the way you must walk your Road.

> We can choose courage, or we can choose comfort, but we can't have both. Not at the same time.[83]
>
> BRENÉ BROWN

DISRUPT YOURSELF DAILY

'Disrupt yourself, big man!' Jimmy shouts.

Jimmy is a mentor, of sorts. A 60-something-year-old Scot, some strange mix of executive coach and inspirational motivator. He is impossibly difficult to decipher (unless you grew up in Dunfermline, by the docks). And yet patently easy to understand. Jimmy greets me in the same way each time.

'Disrupt yourself, big man. Disrupt yourself!'

He stands way too close, too far into my personal space. It's uncomfortable, awkwardly visceral. But for some reason I love it. Jimmy is committed to provoking growth in me, which he knows invariably comes by way of disruption.

'Karl, it's going to take courage!'

Courage to jump, to change, to lead. As I have learned to apply disruption to my leadership, disruption even when it has not been brought about by others or external factors, I have begun to discover a truth that is serving me well. The peace you desire, the security that you would lead from, the growth that, in your best moments, you yearn for, will not be yours unless you stir it up. Almost every

83 Brené Brown, *Daring Greatly: How the Courage to Be Vulnerable Transforms the Way We Live, Love, Parent, and Lead* (Gotham Books, 2012), p71.

opportunity for growth has its roots in disruption; study Nelson Mandela or, in truth, any leader worth following.

In fact, prove it yourself, every day in the middle of the day – choose the way of the Brave.

For me that disruption comes daily in the form of an alarm.

PAUSE – BREATHE – CHOOSE

The smartphone that is never out of reach alerts me at midday, every day. It's inconvenient, shrill and irritating. I'm usually in the middle of something I don't want to be disturbed from. I'm writing, or thinking, or driving. Sometimes the alarm is embarrassing, as I'm in the guts of a difficult work conversation or on a video call coaching session. Always, the non-melodic tone is a disruption.

I guess that's the point. I set the alarm because I want to be disturbed. I want to be shaken out of whatever I'm doing. I'm intentionally resetting my day around my purpose. I alarm my day so I don't sleepwalk through my life. I don't want fireside regrets. I don't want to get to the end of the day having made great agreements with myself in the Cave in the morning that I failed to live out. It's a battle; one I often lose, but one I must fight if I want to grow and lead.

You might use an alarm. You might need a splash of cold water. You might close your screens to check a purpose-aligning paragraph you wrote in your notebook. Take a coffee break. Or a walk around the block. The practice of checking the Road and staying on the path is a recognition that the complexity of the day has a predisposition to steal the intention and focus of its beginning. The alarm I set is just a trigger to get me to pause; it's a small thing but acts as powerful intervention in the war against hurry.

'I'm just a little busy right now.'
'I'm so exhausted, I think it's just the season we are in.'
'I've got so much on my plate, but I just need to get to … year end … holiday … retirement … '
'I feel like I'm shovelling snow in a blizzard.'

Have you noticed how often 'busy' is paraded as a reason for tiredness, or an excuse for missing out on life, or even a badge of honour? I've lived most of my adult life busy. Even my student days were full (from about midday to 2 am). I have come to accept that busy is not the problem, not even the enemy. I'm sure that the nature of a full life with myriad possibilities explored and opportunities taken will be necessarily busy. Our lives are full. If you're holding down a job, maintaining friendships, parenting children and staying cognizant of what is happening in our fast-changing world …

Busy is not our villain. Hurry is.

Hurry has a voice that is shrill, a volume that is hard to ignore. It shouts: Now! Act! Decide! Quick! Choose!

Hurry is when you convince yourself that you can multi-task despite all evidence to the contrary. If you managed it, you would be the first human being to ever accomplish this feat. No one multi-tasks; at best, we juggle. We switch from one energy-focused activity to another.[84] And yet we still try. Several windows open at once. Three items on the daily list due to be closed at the same time.

And so we run out of the house, five minutes late for the meeting we set up, trying not to look at the mobile phone as we drive above the speed limit, calling two people on the way, and pouring coffee down our white shirt as we do.

Rarely does something truly good come from hurry. Decisions made. Work done. Car driven. Words said. Capitulating to it

---

84 A team of researchers from University of California, San Francisco and the University of Pennsylvania conducted fMRI scans and found that when people 'multi-tasked', their brain constantly switched from one task to the other, and ultimately diminished the activity in the prefrontal cortex, which is where the brain makes decisions and holds attention. Study published here: D.S. Ruchkin, et al. (2009). 'Neural correlates of concurrent performance of two cognitive tasks: Evidence from functional magnetic resonance imaging' in *Nature Neuroscience*, 12(2), pp138–144.

happens when we excuse it, rationalize it, or with a resigned shrug, surrender to it.

Hurry is what busy becomes without the discipline of taking a moment to pause, breathe and choose.[85]

Pause ⟶ Breathe ⟶ Choose

When the alarm disrupts, it reminds me to pause; it's a small thing but it's the only way I know to get back on the Road. A simple but necessary circuit breaker, its promise is a reset, its offer is space and its potential is bravery, purpose and focus.

In practice, the pause helps you turn down the volume so you can hear clearly the affirmations you made at the start of the day in the Cave. In truth its greatest strength is to move you from the granular and tactical (in the weeds) to the strategic and significant (lift your head). So please don't rush past this, because your urgency and your hurry is currently and subtly undermining your leadership.

Tactics without strategy just become busy activity, the overflow of acting on what is urgent without selecting what is important. Busy without pause will keep you here and not get you where you want to go; any tactic that loses sight of strategy will limit purposeful impact.

Pausing will help you here. It will give you space to choose; to choose better, deeper, longer, truer. It might not appear to be a momentous thing, but it's the first step in a revolutionary act against the tyranny of the noise and the hurry. It is to decide to engage soul in the process of day.

Arrest the moment! Think back to the Cave. Now forward to the prize. Pause and breathe. Breathe. Take note of your breathing;

---

85 This framework is used by a number of people in the coaching space, including Naz Beheshti, in her book *Pause. Breathe. Choose.: Become the CEO of Your Well-Being* (New World Library, 2021).

your body breathes for you, all the time. Pause and breathe for it. Don't stop reading or switch off. This might sound as if we are entering a kind of hippy, alternative mind shift gear. We aren't. We're becoming aware. So that we can choose.

To breathe in True, Brave, Kind and Curious, first you need to breathe out.

Breathe out hurry.
Breathe in purpose.
Breathe out accidental.
Breathe in intentional. Find cadence here.

Breathe out.
Breathe in.
Breathe out.
Breathe in.

Breathe deeply.

The action of deep breathing is a ruse to slow the hurry of your brain. It gives your brain time to catch up with your intentions. It gives you the chance to take back responsibility for your emotions. Take back control of your thinking, your reacting, your acting. Pause and breathe.

There are so many breathing exercises available these days.

Look them up and pick one.

4-4-4-4 is what I use. It's known as the box breathing technique. (I tried some others but found them too complex, too challenging or I needed to be too fit.)

Breathe in through my nose for 4 seconds. Fill up my lungs.

Hold my breath for 4 seconds.

Breathe out through my mouth for 4 seconds, making a whooshing sound.

Pause for 4 seconds with my lungs empty.

Repeat a couple of times.

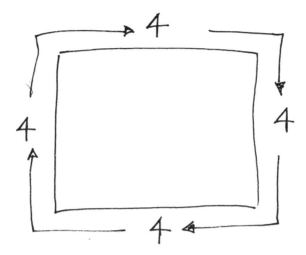

Choose resilience. Choose to keep going. That's a Brave choice.

I GET KNOCKED DOWN, BUT I GET UP AGAIN

A good half of the art of living is resilience.[86]

ALAIN DE BOTTON

Anyone determined to lead from a deeper place, from the soul, will find themselves at times experiencing the loneliness of the leadership walk, the challenge of choosing between people or the heartache of violent disagreement, the frustration of misunderstanding and the agony of rejection. The way of the Brave is to learn to face this head on and walk into it, not run from it.

A wise man once encouraged me to build my leadership shelter before the storm arrived. I took him to mean that I should prepare myself, my mind, my heart, my leadership principles and muscles before they were all tested. And they have been tested! To borrow from Alain de Botton, a good part of leading bravely is to keep on keeping on! Or keep on getting up again.

86 Frequently attributed to Alain de Botton, but not in any of his printed works.

When I was a child, we had limited toy options. We were possibly better off for it. For us, no Playstation or electric scooter: we had chopper bikes and Lego sets. One of the most memorable toys I had was a set of Weebles, made by Hasbro and launched in 1971. They were egg-shaped figures who, as far as I could understand, had no other function apart from their ability to rebound. the counterweight inside the figure meant that no amount of punching, hitting, or throwing could stop them popping back upright again. The marketing strapline was: 'Weebles wobble, but they don't fall down.'

These infeasibly ridiculous, heavy-bottomed plastic toys and their ability to right themselves keep returning to my mind as I coach senior executives. In fact, there are times when it's all I can do to stop myself launching into a cringing commercial jingle. Weebles had a moment, which has passed. And yet there is something extremely fascinating, desirable and even followable about the leader who gets knocked down, but they get up again, one who has grown get-back-up-again muscles. Their moment has not yet passed.

Leaders who get knocked down and get back up again are *great*. Leaders who get knocked down and get back up *better* are *best*. For they have become confident in the midst of chaos and disruption. This quality is described by numerous thinkers as resilience.

Writer and risk analyst, Nassim Nicholas Taleb, coined the term 'antifragile'[87] in his book of the same title, *Antifragile: Things That Gain from Disorder*, to describe certain things which, like bindweed and the human body, seem to gain from disorder: the more pressure or trauma you place upon them, the more they strengthen, grow and prosper.

---

87 Nassim Nicholas Taleb, *Antifragile: Things That Gain From Disorder* (Penguin, 2012). Interestingly, Taleb criticizes academics who fill their work with quotes from others simply to help their friends achieve the tally of how many times their work is quoted elsewhere. He says he hopes his own work will be criticized. I think I can help with that. The irony is that Taleb seems to fill his work with the acerbic criticism of others in order to deflect attention from his disjointed writing and gaps in his thinking. And his work seems to be quoted simply for its title, because it remains unread due to his convoluted and impenetrable style.

Brave leadership is antifragile, perhaps beyond resilient. Courageous leaders not only bounce back, they leap forward, and take great strides along the Road. They remain purposeful and focused in the harshest of environments and grow under the greatest difficulty and persecution. To walk the Road you must learn resilience, perhaps even become antifragile.

But how do you do that? What follows are a few Brave practices that have served me well, I hope they do the same for you:

The Law of 1%

As you lead, you will be criticized. Any leader who leads on purpose, with focus and keeps on moving is implicitly challenging the status quo and the comfort of the known. That will always provoke an attack from the fearful and the comfortable. Expect it. And learn from it. Grow from it. Even when it's unfair. In fact, make the unfair work for you.

In every critique, however harsh or selfish, there will be truth. There is always at least 1% that's fair and can be learned from – I call this the 'Law of 1%'. Embracing this law will grow you. When I've been Brave enough to stand in the full glare of critique and have not retreated to a fortified position of my own correctness, I have grown. Actively look out for the 1% (or more) and embrace it. Spit out the rest.

Q-TIP

Quit Taking It Personally![88] Most attacks that come at you, are not actually about you. Not really.

They owe more to the way someone else is feeling or thinking about themselves and the moment they are experiencing than what you may or may not have done. Their frustration is, likely as not, the overflow of the day they are having, the choices they have made and the struggles of their own leadership pathway. Not taking it personally will help you lead courageously and from your soul.

---

88 Douglas Stone, Bruce Patton, and Sheila Heen, 'Quit Taking It Personally' in *Harvard Business Review*, 1999, volume 77 (issue 1), pp76–83.

However, don't use Q-TIP to abdicate responsibility for dealing with your stuff or addressing the issues you need to in yourself. You're still in the circle.

Never Defend Yourself

I try to lead with this maxim as a rule; it keeps me Brave.

In the guts of leading, when you feel opposed, wounded or upset, there is an almost universal proclivity to defend yourself. Newton's third law of motion is a helpful reference point here: 'For every action there is an equal and opposite reaction.' [89] If you exert a force, it is more than likely that the same force will be exerted in your direction. If you defend, you meet defence.

Listen, you may well have good reason to shut down or posture up. Whenever you do, you compound the problem and further postpone your growth. I have found that becoming defensive cements me into a position from which I find it difficult to move or grow and tends to provoke a 'mirror' reaction in those I perceive to be attacking me. Everyone becomes defensive and nobody wins. The vision is not embraced, the strategy is not advanced, and the team does not perform. Conversely, when I refuse to become defensive, the opportunity for movement on both sides, for learning or for restoration is greatly enhanced. You create space for creative resolution.

'Never defend yourself' does not mean 'shut up' (not always), especially if to be silent means that your non-verbal communication screams 'I'M NOT GOING TO DEFEND MYSELF!' Pause – and take courageous responsibility. Below are some suggestions for navigating could-be defensive moments:

- *Assume comments or actions have been clumsy not intentional*: Often, my experience has been that an attack from someone I've been attempting to lead is not motivated by hatred of me, but fear

89 Isaac Newton, *Mathematical Principles of Natural Philosophy*, translated by Andrew Motte, revised by Florian Cajori. 3rd ed, (University of California Press, 1962), p34.

of change, or misunderstanding of my motives. (There will be times when the attack is purely malicious. If it is, suck it up. Take it on the chin and close the conversation as quickly as possible.)

- *Name your wrong*: They need you to admit fault where there is fault. Fess up – sometimes that alone releases the pressure valve. Courage is often less about forging forward with a fresh and radical idea and more about rowing back from a position you have taken or made a stand on, that is wrong, unhelpful or ungenerous. 'Sorry, I might be wrong,' is one of the most powerful leadership sentences. Never employ it as a tactic, but when it's the truth, run to it.

- *Clarify*: They need you to clarify your motive, with grace. They need to know why you did what you did and what you meant to achieve – no more, no less.

- *Leverage Loss*: Never waste a crisis. It is widely reported, although not substantiated, that when Winston Churchill was working to form the United Nations after World War II, he made the statement, 'Never let a good crisis go to waste.'[90] Whether he did or not, it's great advice. Don't abuse the crisis for your own ends, but redeem it for all it's worth.

I can easily bring to mind my own mini-crises – failures of vision and ideas; face plants of strategies and tactics – more than I would care to list here and all my own fault and of my own making. Staff hired too quickly and let go too slowly. Money spent that we shouldn't have. Changes made that were ineffective. I'm sure you have many stories of your own, just don't let them go to waste.

Sometimes all you can do is survive in the storm. And if you survive the storm, you can thrive after the storm. All the best opportunities come later.

90 The earliest time this was referenced and attributed to Churchill in publication was 1934 in Raymond Moley's book *The New Deal: A Modern Myth*; Moley had been a political advisor to President Franklin D. Roosevelt.

If you do this work and keep on going, you will have developed 'standing in the storm' muscles and a 'standing in the storm' story that can be passed on. You will have experience and confidence that can be leveraged. I can now help people in trauma, because I've been there; I can process rejection and help others experiencing it, because I didn't deny it and am still standing despite it. I am also a living testimony to the truth that you can fail repeatedly, and it doesn't make you a failure, but it does offer you a springboard to help you win and raise those who will fail and then succeed.

MAKING COURSE CORRECTIONS

There are times when, halfway down the Road, even if you set out with clear purpose and focus, you will find yourself lost or stuck, even walking the wrong way. You need to course correct. It can be truly foolish to keep on going at an enterprise that is failing or misguided without asking some questions. There are moments when it is less about keeping going in the belief that it will all work out and more about facing down the reality of the moment you find yourself in. The diagnosis needed on the Road is not simply the truth of self-awareness, it is at the same time situational awareness.

You will need to pause, *reflectively*, so you may act, *decisively*. Stop to clarify the options and then to prune them. What is True about where I am? What are the brutal facts about the success or failure of my current moment? What are the directional options open to me now?

Brave leaders ask the right question: what is the wise thing to do? It is a question that is joined at the hip with your purpose and your focus. Not, firstly, what is the expedient thing to do? Or what is the expected course of action here? Certainly not, what is the safe thing to do? Look at the facts, pay attention to your feelings, write them down. In my coaching practice, we employ three questions borrowed from the normative arc of storytelling:

What is? What could be? What will be?[91]
Or:
Reality? Possibility? Opportunity?

Face the reality of the situation in front of you – do your own work on this. Now do the truly Brave thing: ask for help. Employ the wisdom of other eyes, minds and hearts to help you see.

'I'm moving forward, here is my thinking, what do you think is the right next step?'
Expect pushback, in fact ask for it.

'Tell me what is wrong with my current plan?'

'Ipcha mistabra' – The best translation of this Aramaic phrase, adopted by Israeli intelligence after the 1973 Yom Kippur War, is 'on the contrary it appears that'. It describes a posture and practice their forces universally adopted. It also formed the backbone of the job specification of their 'Red Teams,' the experts brought in to analyse and appraise every plan about to be undertaken.

Popular psychology often references this practice as 'the 10th man principle,' the sworn responsibility in a room of peers, when there is universal agreement over a course of action. The tenth or last person to speak must oppose, play devil's advocate, and disagree. This principle of dissent has saved many bad ventures from launching and corrected many mistakes that would have had destructive outcomes.

Unless you make space for 'on the contrary it appears that' conversations, your leadership will flounder.

The way of the Brave is the Road less travelled. It's disruptive,

91 Stephen Denning, *The Leader's Guide to Radical Management: Reinventing the Workplace for the 21st Century* (Jossey-Bass, 2010) p25.

disturbing and costly. Above all it requires intention to walk it. To arrest the day, pause – breathe – choose, and to keep going, keep on getting up and staying the course.

You may think it's not possible for you to be so wholehearted, purposeful, resilient, decisive and focused.

I might answer 'Ipcha mistabra.'

'On the contrary it appears that' … it is.

THE CAVE

THE ROAD

THE FIRE

THE TABLE

CHAPTER 7

THE TABLE:
the art of the Kind

A TALE OF TWO TABLES

In the boardroom of the corporate headquarters of one of my clients, two of the four walls are glass, floor to ceiling, and look out over a cityscape of sky-reaching buildings, neon signs and streets below. The other two walls are filled with screens, whiteboards and motivational art. There is, on hand, a friendly and brilliant IT technician, whose primary job is to make certain all connections. Which is good because that's the point of the Table.

The table is immaculate, shiny dark wood resin; the perfect surface to slide a contract across, to push an idea around, or to stand over, reserved, with arms folded or with fingertips expressively splayed on the veneer to intimidate a colleague or client. The legs are shiny chrome and the roller-wheeled chairs less comfortable and stable than their promise. This table hosts strategy conversations, marketing pitches and cultural reboots around its angular form. It is a place where commitments are requested, resolutions announced; it is a place of hirings and firings.

In my conservatory, three of the four walls are glass, floor to ceiling, but each small pane is held in place by white painted Victorian-style astragals. They look out over beech and willow, peonies and dahlias. The internal wall is largely open to the kitchen, but the exposed pillars of pink sandstone are hung with collections of art, floppy hats and plaid rugs. The table is heavy and formed from ancient oak, rich with scars and red wine rings that tell of gatherings and connection.

Surrounding the table are eight mismatched smoker's bow chairs, which have seen many hard years of service in an English pub, now furnished with cushions. They provide just the right balance of comfort and rigidity that persuades diners to linger and talk.

These tables are real; you can pull up a chair, sit around them and talk. And what is equally real is what they stand for and all that is achieved around them. Two tables. Two rooms. Entirely different. Yet they share essence, crucial opportunities and functions: the health of your business and my business, the well-being of your family and my family, is largely contingent on what occurs as we sit in these spaces. And how we do so.

Soul Leadership needs both Tables.

At the Table, we connect. We communicate. We attend to our relationships. To others. And in doing so, to our own soul. That is why the Table is a space of kindness, it's what makes the Table sacred.

This practice of the Table is at heart the discipline of provoking and fostering conversation and connection. And cooperation.

This is a necessary and vital prescription. We're living through an epoch in which we have largely traded intentional time in conversation around tables – being inspired and pouring out our souls – for disconnected virtual meetings or vapid entertainment, slouching passive around blinking screens.

There's a show called *Gogglebox*,[92] where you watch other people watching television, eating snacks and commenting on what they are seeing. Our culture might finally have reached the bottom of the pit it has dug for itself. Watching people and commentating on people watching people comment on people! Have we got nothing better to do with our lives?! And yet, it's totally compelling – and now award-winning. It's so popular that at least fifteen countries outside the UK have their own versions. We mirror them as we criticize them and then award them.

92 Stephen Lambert, Tania Alexander, and Tim Harcourt, 'Gogglebox,' Channel 4, 2013–present day.

Ferenc Máté, in his book *A Real Life*,[93] references a study undertaken by the University of Michigan:[94]

Analyzing the personality tests of 13,737 college students over a 30-year period, between 1979 and 2009, the researchers found a 48 percent decrease in empathy and a 34 percent decrease in perspective-taking – considering someone else's point of view.

His explanation:

Think of this new generation that grew up with remote controls and video games, web surfing and tweeting, constantly distracted, and often overloaded. When did it have time to form complex memories? When did it have time to rest, think deeply, reflect? And when did it have time to feel compassion, sympathy, not to mention empathy? This survey suggests 'almost never.'

The researchers marked an inflection point of greatest change right around the year 2000, which brought the 'inundation of callous reality TV shows, and the explosion of social networks and texting.' The world in which *Gogglebox* is a massive hit.

I believe that it is at the Table – how we emphasize it, who we gather around it, and how we talk beside it – where we will rediscover empathy, connectedness and a kinder form of leadership.

I'm not saying don't watch TV. I am saying do talk. To real people, with real intention.

I'm not saying don't work remotely. I am saying make every effort, whenever you can, to do face to face, in a room with real people.

Above all, I am saying, lay a Table.

93 Ferenc Máté, *A Real Life* (Knopf, 2011), pp14–15.
94 Jean M. Twenge and W. Keith Campbell, 'The Narcissism Epidemic: Living in the Age of Entitlement' (Free Press, 2009).

While practising the way of the Brave, walking the Road involves a mid-journey checkpoint to turn off the noise; coming to the Table is about welcoming noise to widen your perspective with the counsel you need, in order to lead well. It is also the kindest place to have the sort of conversations that resolve disagreement, reinforce resolutions, redirect efforts or redeem lost causes.

Come to the Table as often as you can; it will serve you well. Don't eat lunch on your own.

TABLE DYNAMICS

'No Andrew, can you sit over there; Jill, could you move up here?'

Nick is as much a composer or conductor as he is a chairman, in truth that's why he is so good at his role. Nick sometimes has a table seating map, where he would like his team to sit; he always has a conversation and conflict plan, how he wants the discussion to go, where the roadblocks will be and how the team might remove them.

Nick chairs the board of a successful manufacturing company. Recently, he was leading his team through a private-equity-funded acquisition of a competitor. He leads his Table with forensic forethought, part conductor but all planner, he approaches every meeting as if he was working through a complex, challenging but beautiful symphony. He sees the provoking and the managing of conflict as a significant part of the musical composition, albeit with a pen and not a baton in hand.

If you were part of Nick's team you would rarely stumble across conflict; it would, in truth, be predicted and war-gamed pre-Table and then played out at the Table. He spends almost three times as long in the planning for the Table as it takes to lead at the Table. This is where his strength comes from.

At the same time, Nick possesses a supreme and seemingly instinctive skill to bring different voices into the conversation at precisely the right moments. He knows who needs time to think deeply (mostly his introverts), and who should be allowed to talk so that they can process (mostly his extroverts). He is also smart enough to not take too seriously the first opinions of the verbal processors, allowing them to work their thinking through aloud. If you were to statistically analyze the airtime each voice is given in the boardroom you would find a staggering equality; this is, in no way, accidental. If you find yourself thinking that Nick had read Amy Edmondson's work on psychological safety[95] in a team and was applying it, literally, you would be correct – but the same could be said of almost any other team leadership study you could name here. In fact, the spontaneity with which Nick appears to lead is not accidental; he wants to lead with fairness, safety, trust and relationship so he studies to and plans to.

Nick reads, pushes and leads his Table deliberately and resolutely. If you sat with him and talked, he would probably tell you that his kindness is not naturally relational – for him kindness is clarity and clarity is what Nick does best.

The size and place of a family dining table has developed over time: as you sit around it, you are both across from and beside one another, close enough to talk easily, just far enough for personal space. The head of the table is traditionally a place of authority – that's generally where a parent sits. There is something edible to give your attention to: in my native Scotland it might be haggis and neeps, perhaps even a cranachan.[96] The family dining table is a place of culture and ritual, cooperation and conflict. There are rules, spoken and unspoken, and a complex system of manners – don't speak with your mouth full, don't bolt your food, don't be late. The rules may be challenged or broken – there might be emotional

95 Amy C. Edmondson, *The Fearless Organization: Creating Psychological Safety in the Workplace for Learning, Innovation, and Growth* (Wiley, 2018).
96 For those unfamiliar with these delicacies, haggis – the national dish of Scotland – is a pudding that traditionally includes the liver, heart, and lungs of a sheep, minced and mixed with beef, onions and spices, then packed into a sheep's stomach and boiled. Neeps are boiled and mashed turnips. Cranachan is a dessert with oats, raspberries, whisky and cream. Don't knock them 'til you've tried them.

outbursts, sometimes suppressed tension. It is said that this is the place that power dynamics are first learned.

In the boardroom there are a comparable set of rules, culture and ritual. In the centre there might be a carafe of water, perhaps coffee and biscuits on the sideboard. The menu is the agenda and the meat is in the reports, with AOB instead of dessert, but there are comparable rules and the breaking of them – address the chair, don't interrupt, keep on topic, disagree well and commit.

WELL-LAID TABLES EXPAND THINKING

If you fail to come to the Table, to regularly meet with your people, you are in danger of becoming little more than a caricature of your best opinions or worst ideas. Thought leaders who dwell in echo chambers are limited. Even the keenest minds will run out of fresh and productive thought and will stagnate around old ideas, if deprived of challenge and check, response and push back. The vitality of your leading is contingent on the freshness of your thinking, and the freshness of your thinking is dependent on the rebuttal and reframing that flows from a curated Table.

The best Soul Leaders have thought partners. But your virtual guru can rarely be a good thought partner. A message on your phone is not a conversation around a Table. A sound bite is not a discourse. Input from your Insta psychologist or your most-read author is useful, but if they are not at the Table, they cannot be 'bread fellows' and will not be there in the moments, the details and the contexts that truly count. Expecting these advisors to become your check up, your push back or your schooling can be dangerous.

Coaches are important, but it's the people you welcome around your Table and how you talk with them, the teammates you trust with your thinking, who will really hone your ideas, perspectives and judgments and shape your life.

The Table has a unique magic that can enable us to feel known, seen, heard and understood, yielding both constraints and possibilities that don't restrict us but rather free us.

We need people to say, 'Yes, and … ' as a cautionary check, and 'Yes, and … ' as a challenging nudge. To say, 'Have you thought about the probable results of the thoughts you're espousing?' To say, 'Have you considered the opposite approach to the solution you're actioning?' And as a push to dream bigger, to say, 'Do you realize what you might be missing out on? Are you aware of this opportunity you might be currently blind to?'

When our Table companions become collaborators and co-conspirators their questions offer perspective and round off our thinking. When the needs and thoughts of those around us become as important as the ambitions or agenda within us we open ourselves up to fresh thinking and possibilities.

CONFLICT AT THE TABLE

If Tables were made for connection, and if connection is forged by conversation, those Tables might just come into their own in moments of potential or real disagreement. The art of the Kind is often played out in the arena of conflict.

Conflict and kindness are not usually regarded as close companions or taught in the same module in most MBAs – but I believe they belong in the same conversation. For any leader who seeks to bring about regular, effective and healthy change, the ability to engage regular, effective and healthy conflict is paramount. It's at the heart of leading kindly.

The Table is the most obvious vehicle for these sort of conversations, coming to it well and leading it skilfully may well be the deciding factor in whether you manage healthy teams. Or not.

There was a sharp disagreement, the room was hot, the air was heavy and tension was rising. Two protagonists looked at each other warily. She addressed them both:

'We know you currently disagree; I'm not sure continuing to do so in this room is going to help our cause. I know that the likelihood of agreement as you debate it here is remote. Would you consider taking this offline for thirty minutes and attempt to answer this question: "for the sake of aiding in the crisis before us, can we imagine a compromise position that can get us collaborating at the speed we need to?"'

They returned with an agreed path that moved the organization forward. Unafraid of issuing the corporate equivalent of a time out, Andrea runs her global non-profit, leading, reading and pushing her Table with graceful brilliance. The success she has with unpaid but highly qualified volunteers on her board in navigating complex and volatile situations is unquestionable. Getting aid into war-torn Ukraine while also evacuating aid workers, housing a deluge of refugees from Syria and teaching their children are among many responses her organization is lauded for. It's what she does around the Table that is for me most remarkable.

It's her navigation of boardroom conflict that enables all that happens in the field to make all the difference in the world. Her superpower is relationships. She knows her board members, she understands who gets stressed about what, who will react and how, who she must talk to before meetings, who needs a longer 'on ramp' to decision and who is comfortable with 'in the moment' consideration. Andrea's boardroom Table is successful because her dining room Table is. The capital she gains as she breaks bread, drinks shiraz and talks family is the capital she spends as she challenges mindsets, asks for larger spends than seems possible and moves quickly to bold and brave decisions. Andrea is masterful at using her relational capital to push the board just beyond their normal comfort to get them to where they need to be.

In moments around the Table where trust is broken between members, I have yet to see trust broken between Andrea and anyone else; what I have seen is her use that trust to broker resolution.

You will find many worthwhile models and resources to help with conflict management and mediation. (Kenneth Thomas and

Ralph Kilmann developed a conflict resolution model that we use often.[97]) What follows is not designed to be an in-depth or even exhaustive study in navigating conflict but rather a provocation to allow or acknowledge some conflict and a cheat sheet in doing it kindly. I have found three actions helpful:

1. Know the Table

Know where you and others default to in conflict or under pressure. Now ask yourself if there is a better conversation that could be had:

- Do you need to win at all costs? What if the desire to win is the greatest roadblock to progress or health?
- Do you bury your head in the sand when any need for confrontation arises?
- Do you try to please the other person in the conversation to the extent that you always lose?
- Do you settle for compromise as a good enough solution? Or could we press on through to find a better way, together?

Knowing where they are and where you go to is the first step to a Kind challenging of positions and a courageous move toward solution.

2. Push the Table

Avoidance is ultimately a dead zone. It is interesting that this posture that appears, at first glance, the kindest, is actually the least Kind. On almost every occasion that I have brushed a problem under the carpet or refused to confront conduct that is inappropriate it has either become a bigger issue than it needed to be or come back to bite me later.

97 The Thomas-Kilmann Conflict Model Instrument (TKI) was developed by Kenneth Thomas and Ralph Kilmann in 1974 as a self-assessment, measuring how people tend to respond within a conflict.

Put the issue on the Table, name it simply and dispassionately, refuse to take offense and be sure to not give it.

Now encourage an open debate.

3. Lead the Table

All roads to resolution go through compromise. What are we willing to lose, that we might all gain? Compromise is progress, but it is not usually the best end game – that is collaboration. To push on through at the Table, we might ask ourselves two further questions:

- Can we articulate a purpose that is bigger than any of our personal wins?
- Are we willing to search for a solution that none of us has currently thought of?

Practising the two Tables is about making your boardroom Table relational and your dining Table intentional and about blurring the lines when you can.

THE BOARDROOM TABLE

There are many objections that can be made to the intimacy I'm suggesting here. There are boundary conversations to be had, and yet, few of those possible objections are more compelling than the potential available for the team that learns to be a community and the wisdom that grows from the vulnerable coming together at the Table.

I mentioned that I write into many of my contracts a non-negotiable: I would like to take your team out for dinner, a private room, good food and wine, and I reserve the right to set the Table question. Everyone plays; there are no observers, just participants.

One of my favourite questions is:

'What is the greatest contribution this person brings to the team? Be specific with real-life examples. What do you long to see more of in this regard?'

I have spent many long evenings leaning in, laughing and moved to tears by the revelations and encouragements that pour out of the conversation provoked by this question. I've also had the privilege of watching a team flourish in the aftermath of the affirmations embraced and trust gained from intentional meal moments like this. They move forward changed.

So, sit down with your team; lay the Table for them. Eat together. Break bread. Lead it well. Have great conversations. Don't fill the Table with talk: fill it with the learnings of life. Fill it with interest and debate. Fill it with a little bit of a wrestle about issues that personally impact the lives present.

A Kind conversation has three coherent parts: curated conflict (as just discussed), great listening and keen questioning.

Great Listening

Very few people truly listen well. Listen to listen, not just to respond. If you listen to respond, you won't hear the heart, the nuance, the question in the statement.

As I reflect on years of sitting around boardroom tables or away with my team on vision retreats, my strongest critique would be 'too much talk; not enough wisdom'. Open mouths and closed minds. Leaders who spend their time between bouts of talking, thinking about what to say next. Leaders eagerly seizing on someone else's words purely as the excuse for talking themselves. Listen to listen; not only is it respectful and Kind but you will learn.

There are at least three levels of listening: superficial, selective and empathetic.[98]

---

98 Often attributed to Carl Rogers, one of the founders of humanistic psychology.

1. SUPERFICIAL.

2. SELECTIVE.

3. * EMPATHIC .*

Only number three is really listening. Listen so you can connect: with another person's thoughts, feelings and leadership perspective; speaking only to understand what it is like, what it feels like and what it could be like to be in their seat. Lean in and look at the speaker. Don't interrupt; allow them to finish. Repeat what they have said in your own words; show how you've understood.

Listening for all of that is Kind. Then, and only then, when you have done all that, respond. By asking great questions.

Keen Questions

One of my closest friends is a successful lawyer and a world-class question ninja. He has many gifts, but this is an art he's perfecting. I've been at multiple gatherings that have sparkled, not just because of the food and wine, but, in truth, because of the questions asked and the way they were asked. The Table he lays with the curiosity he carries enables conversations that touch your soul.

One of the best moments of my parenting life was enabled when I visited this friend, and he lent me his car and booked a table at one of the best restaurants in town for my family (generosity is another world-class gift that his wife and he carry). As we left for the meal, he handed me an envelope. 'Read this as you start dessert,' he said. The envelope had a short list of questions, which we were to ask one another. What followed was the opening up of true conversation, the deepening of real relationship and the much-needed release of emotion. As we ate burgers and fries, s'mores and ice cream, overlooking a deep pink Pacific sunset, we laughed until it hurt, wept and connected in a new way.

We all remember it as if it were yesterday and live in the overflow of it. Even now. Listen, really listen; please don't reserve these profound moments for immediate family, these moments are the stuff of which all great partnerships, all great companies are made.

The best teams eat together. And not just a rushed sandwich in a squeezed lunch hour, but a quiet room, with a curated moment, and an intentional interaction. I believe you will find that the overflow of such experiences will have more impact than many board meetings around office tables or strategy sessions outworked on whiteboards.

Host a Table experience for your team that takes you beyond task, goal and process. Lay it monthly and intentionally. Open your house or hire a private room, and approach it as if it is the most strategic gathering of that month. It might just be.

Ask a question or two.

Great questions are open questions, questions that encourage people to elaborate, provocations that promise insight into them as a person. For example:

What is the most important lesson you learned from your family?
Looking back over your life, what would you describe as your proudest moment?
If you owned this company, what one rule would you change?
If you could change roles with anyone around this table, who would it be and why?

Try to see your questions as the start of a conversation that could end up who knows where. Ask follow ups, not as an inquisitor or a counsellor, but as a collaborator and as a friend. For example:

Can you tell me more?
How so?
How did that make you feel?
What did you learn from that?
What do you plan to do as a result?

Listen for responses. Catalyze the kindness and curiosity in the room.

DINING TABLE

A quaich is a traditional Scottish drinking vessel – a cup of metal, wood or bone with a handle on each side, designed to carry a drink to be shared.[99]

For centuries of highland history, the head of two clans would sip whisky from a quaich as a vulnerable act of trust and bonding, sometimes commemorating a strategic marriage, or an alliance, between their tribes.

So when one of my daughters got married, we marked the moment with communal sips of the local distillation, a *Glenkinchie 15*, as a symbolic way of joining two families together. It's physical; it's kinetic; it's Kind to share in this way. While ceremonial sips, in life, are rightly few and far between, we can embrace and evoke the essence of the quaich whenever we sit for a meal together, and *how* we do so.

When you eat – as often as you can, do so with others. And talk; move on from the idle chatter of the gossip columns or the trending streams, towards a meaningful insight into the lives of those who do life with you, have done life before you, and want life for you.

99 John MacInnes, *The Quaich: A Symbol of Friendship and Collaboration* (Birlinn, 2013).

Make your relationships intentional. It might be a snapshot of the activity of the day, each day. Or a deeper curated conversation, weekly, or monthly.

The Daily Table

We eat simple food most evenings, but we do it together, resisting as much as possible the temptation to eat on a lap with a screen for company. I ask three basic questions and everyone gets to answer. Highs, Lows and Grows.

> *'The high point of my day was … '* This is an opportunity for celebration.
> *'The low point of my day was … '* This is an opportunity for empathy.
> *'The growth point of my day was … '* This creates an opportunity for learning.

We don't debate or engage in significant comment, nor do we sit in silent judgment. We listen, to commiserate with the bad, celebrate the good and talk about the growth. You don't need to reserve this just for home; lunchtime at work might be just as impactful.

The Weekly Table

The key to meaningful dinner parties is intention; you plan a menu, a seating plan, a table layout – in the same way curate your conversation.

Listen to Priya Parker in her brilliant work, *The Art of Gathering: How We Meet and Why It Matters*:

> *Gatherings crackle and flourish when real thought goes into them, when (often invisible) structure is baked into them, and when a host has the curiosity, willingness, and generosity of spirit to try.*[100]

100 Priya Parker, *The Art of Gathering: How We Meet and Why It Matters* (Riverhead Books, 2018), p6.

This Table is likely to be a room full of your friends – or those who will become your friends. These are people you wish to do life with and want to grow with; people who may share a common philosophy but have different perspectives. These are your people. Sometimes you'll want to also include some friends who are currently in your 'marketplace'. It's the vibrant combination of both consistent and fresh voices that make this ritual energizing.

As you prepare The Table:

- *Set it for comfort*: We bought our smoker's bow chairs and cushions because with our previous seats we noticed that one hour in, everyone was fidgeting. We provide great food and wine, because a quality conversation is fuelled by a quality meal.
- *Keep it focused*: One conversation at a time, or else the dinner party becomes cliquey, people feel left out, wisdom and hilarity is wasted and some personalities can dominate the atmosphere.
- *Make it inclusive*: As a host, your job is to read the room and facilitate the conversation in a way that involves everyone. The extroverts in the room will need to articulate their thoughts in order to work out what they're thinking – they need to be given time and space to do so. Any idea that the extrovert firmly believes the first iteration of their thought would be a foolish assumption – however passionately it is expressed in the room – they are usually just testing it out. Don't hold them to it. Introverts will need thinking time to confidently share their thoughts. Sharing the question early will always pay dividends. It will often be the case that those who are more reflective will need their thoughts, comments and humour drawn out from them.

The skilful host will lead the Table discussion like an expert conductor – bringing each part in at the right time, knowing how to allow for silence and discord.

While there is a huge benefit from the informality of easy relationship, the kindness of this Table time is discovered on the far side of a framework or rules of engagement.

The reason I'm advocating for rules is that the benefits of your Table will almost always be undermined by three things: experts, soapboxes and conclusions.

No experts: The best and freest of conversations flow from environments where people take conversation seriously and themselves less so. At our weekly Table, there are no experts allowed, for we are all learners, and all curious. Posturing as an 'expert' tends to shut down most opportunities to learn and grow. At the same time, others in the room are usually more hesitant in proffering an opinion when the expert is there.

No soapboxes: A conversation is always diminished when it collapses into a lecture. At the same time, a lecture is always enhanced when it becomes a conversation. There is, of course, nothing wrong with someone having a strong and well-thought-through opinion, or even getting on their soapbox about it; it's just that the Table is not the place or time for this. Breaking bread is a space for exchanging thoughts, testing ideas and listening to hearts. In its purest fashion, the Table leaves a sliver in the mind which stays open long after being cleared of wine glasses when the night is done.

No conclusions: The pressure to come to conclusion or agreement is understandable, but will usually force a conversation to a goal or an end that is not necessary. The Table is not the debating chamber or the despatch box. Removing the possibility of consensus as the aim gives a freedom to the Table that would otherwise not be there. The gracious skill of making space for your friends to change their minds is an art form rarely cultivated, yet when it is, it offers unprecedented growth opportunities. With these parameters in place, there is freedom to ask deeper questions:

What is disturbing you this week?
What is frustrating you most right now?
What one cultural problem do you wish you could solve and how would you do it?
How could we make our community life stronger and what would it take?

I was always taught that Kind conversations should avoid: politics, faith and money.

I vehemently disagree. Handled well, these conversations are the very stuff of life, the core of many of our leadership decisions, and are in desperate need of Table wisdom. Talk away, but insist on Kind listening and Kind questioning. And see what results.

It is impossible to overstate the importance of the opportunities made available by the right kind of Tables. The Table is a revolt against the dumbing down of our relational worlds, an overture of true connection in a culture desperately in need of it. It may well be the greatest medicine on offer for the current wisdom malaise we're experiencing; the greatest counter to loop thinking and isolation that is sabotaging the potential of Soul Leadership.

So, whether it's a boardroom or a dining room, a coffee or a glass of water, sushi or a sandwich, a buffet or a banquet, takeout on a fold-out, five courses or one. Or no food, just talk … practice the Table.

The practice of the Table is the art of the Kind.

CHAPTER 8

KIND:
at the Table

We have developed speed, but we have shut ourselves in. Machinery that gives us abundance has left us in want. Our knowledge has made us cynical, our cleverness hard and unkind. We think too much and feel too little. More than machinery we need humanity. More than cleverness we need kindness … [101]

CHARLIE CHAPLIN'S CHARACTER IN *THE GREAT DICTATOR* (1940)

Be kind, for everyone you meet is fighting a hard battle.[102]

PLATO

It is the small things, everyday deeds of ordinary folk, that keeps the darkness at bay. Simple acts of kindness and love.[103]

GANDALF IN *THE HOBBIT: AN UNEXPECTED JOURNEY* (2013)

My nephew recently joined the fire service in the UK. The physicality of the job, the life-changing difference he is able to make and the possibility and variety of each shift is just right for him. And during each shift, the team eats together. Not just sandwiches purchased from a nearby deli or soup brought from home, but a full meal, ingredients bought locally, cooked by those who will eat it and enjoyed with conversation around a table by all. It is, in fact, a sacred

101 Chaplin, Charlie, director, *The Great Dictator* (United Artists, 1940), final speech.
102 Most often attributed to Plato; sometimes attributed to Socrates and others.
103 This quotation appears only in the movie, not the book by JRR Tolkien. Peter Jackson, et al. *The Hobbit: An Unexpected Journey* (New Line Productions, 2013), scene 10.

ritual; to prepare together, to eat, talk and clear the plates is a non-negotiable rhythm. They practise the Table.

It's carrying on a tradition. It's controlling nutrition. And it's something more. If you are going to run into a burning building to rescue another human being and risk your life in the process, you must trust in the team around you to have your back and play their part. Eating together strengthens connection; it makes you a team. Those who eat together, firefight together – *for* each other. Breaking bread does that for them. As does eating bacon, sausage and fried eggs!

This practice has huge overspill into their lives. Family connections are made, camping trips enjoyed and sporting challenges are taken together. Those who sit together, talk together, agree together *also* speculate together, learn together and lose and win together. The Table teams are the ones who overcome; it has always been so.

Key to the success of these Table conversations is that we sit, listen and talk with kindness. The space is the Table – the quality is Kind.

> *'Diego, how is your mom? Anna, great to see you again, I thought you only worked on a Friday? How is the tennis coming ... tournament this weekend?'*

We had just arrived at his golf club and as we walked past at least a dozen young adults – some employed for the summer, others starting their working life – Jack had paused at each one. He knew something personal about every one of them; he asked them about how they were, their homelife, college courses and called them by name. They lit up as he did so.

Weeks before, Jack had explained one of his core leadership principles. 'Karl, the most important person on the planet is always the person standing right in front of you.' In those moments, when someone is eyeball to eyeball with you or sitting next to you, if they truly believe that not only do they have your full attention, but that you are genuinely interested in them and that nothing, right now, is more important to you, your ability to influence them, to encourage them, to move them and enable them is remarkable.

His role and success at the very top of one of the largest vehicle manufacturers on the planet doesn't mean he no longer troubles himself with these small gestures. In fact, they are more important than ever – because his leadership is built on this quality; it owes more to 'he knows my name' than almost anything else. Being Kind is the character quality that underpins his career.

I want it to be mine too. Increasingly, the leadership epitaph I would love to have is just that; 'he was kind.' I have come to realize that Kind is strong. It does not indicate a lack of focus or ambition; rather, this powerful leadership trait is deeply motivating, truly liberating, and entirely necessary for the type of high-performing team you want to lead. It is also a trait that is universally needed, for if you would lead there will always be a team in need of kindness.

WE, NOT I

There is no such thing as an individual leader. Just as there is no such thing as an individual sport, there is only team. There is no such thing as a 'company of one', or a sole trader or a one-man band or a solo artist. That might be what it says on the tin, but when you lift the lid, what is revealed is team.

Tiger Woods has a team, as does Rory McIlroy. Their teams are coaches and physios, branding managers and accountants, caddies and friends. Lewis Hamilton has mechanics, agents and personal trainers. In Serena Williams' corner was a coach, Patrick Mouratoglou, a hitting partner, personal rapper (Drake) and a Yorkshire terrier (Chip). My niece is married to a very well-known baseball star; he plays for a Galactico franchise, but employs his own team of a personal nutritionist, marketing agent and sponsors.

Teams are the building blocks of our society: family, community, neighbourhood, political party, athletic club, conservation society, executive board, work cohort. All are teams. And most are under threat.

It feels like team has come to mean less than team. Sports players swap hometown clubs for rivals with bigger budgets. Politicians cross the floors of houses to play for whichever group will get it done. Families break up at alarming rates. Jobs which used to be for life are now for a season. We volunteer until it no longer works well in our schedule. Extended communities are increasingly transient. We don't stay long anymore.

Ironically, while dedication to one team is on the wane, 'kindness' appears to be in vogue: as a feel-good phrase plastered on tote bags, T-shirts and surfboard-encumbered campervans. And yet, there is more to 'kindness' than a hashtag. True kindness is rare: the type of kindness that sees people, honours them, makes space for them to play their part and sacrifices for a bigger cause. The art of the Kind is the basis of team and one of the key characteristics of a sustainable high-performance culture. True, Brave, Curious and Kind.

Research by APEX (Association of Professional Executives of the Public Service of Canada)[104] indicates that kindness has a measurable impact on productivity, finding that teams who are Kind to one another:

- Possess 26% more energy
- Are 30% more likely to feel motivated by new ideas and enthusiastic about acquiring new skills
- Express 36% more satisfaction with their jobs
- Are 44% more committed to their organizations

104 Christine Pearson and Christine Porath, *The Cost of Bad Behavior: How Incivility at Work Drains Morale and Productivity* (Portfolio Publishing, 2009).

THE STRENGTH OF THE WOLF IS THE PACK

Changing sports but not the point, Phil Jackson was one of the greatest basketball coaches in history; coach of the Chicago Bulls from 1989 to 1998, he led them to six NBA championships. In his book *Sacred Hoops: Spiritual Lessons of a Hardwood Warrior*,[105] he describes how he managed the greatest basketball player on the planet, Michael Jordan, by quoting Rudyard Kipling and his 'Law of the Jungle':[106]

> Now this is the law of the jungle, as old and as true as the sky. And the wolf that shall keep it may prosper, but the wolf that shall break it must die. As the creeper that girdles the tree trunk, the law runneth forward and back; For the strength of the pack is the wolf and the strength of the wolf is the pack.

His story was about developing a team mentality and culture, while harnessing the abilities of a man who could sometimes, seemingly, win on his own. What Jackson knew was that the team would not win championships unless they learned to be a team. Jordan could not do it alone.

Helping Jordan become a better player was one part of his job; helping Jordan help the team become a better team was the job. That is also yours. There is no lone wolf leader worth following. The team is your job. Being Kind appears to get it done.

PEOPLE BEFORE PROFIT

I'm sure you've heard this phrase;[107] you've probably used it. It's an aspiration often articulated in progressive organizations. It's not

105 Phil Jackson and Hugh Delehanty, *Sacred Hoops: Spiritual Lessons of a Hardwood Warrior* (Hyperion, 1995), p74.
106 Rudyard Kipling, 'The Law of the Jungle', *The Jungle Book* (Macmillan, 1895), p24.
107 This phrase is thought to have originated by labour leaders amidst the Industrial Revolution in the early nineteenth century.

unusual to come across it, embossed in internal company handouts, enshrined in business value statements or even in branding slogans heralding organizational health.

What I have observed is that while this slogan as a value is almost never a con – even if, on some occasions, it can seem just another tactic to get ahead in the game – it's a hard aspiration to deliver on. Not too challenging, in theory, when the market is up and the firm is winning, but in practice, and when under pressure, the 'stress-testing' of this popular slogan usually exposes something less than Kind.

And yet, it's more than possible to be Kind and successful. In fact, the very best organizations know you can't separate these thoughts. They wrestle with how to be Kind even when it would be expedient to ditch the thought. Over time, the organizations that carry these thoughts in tension make better, more sustainable ROI while being the kind of place you want to work, the type of company you would want to represent.

I'm thinking of one of the most inspirational, entrepreneurial leaders in Scotland, owner of the fastest-growing car dealership business in the country. He gets this principle. In the world of selling cars, the customer is king. But in this company, the team is also king. Not because he wants to give his customers anything other than a royal experience, but because he knows he will not be able to do so on a consistent basis, with scalable possibilities, unless his team is honoured with kindness. So, he focuses on providing a world-class work environment and a Kind team experience.

It is not unusual for a company to offer tailored career paths for all employees, or charity serving opportunities in working hours, or even family fun days for the wider company. But in my experience, it is unique to be doing all these things as a matter of priority. It is not unusual for a business to give donations to good causes, but every year this business gives 10% of its profits to children's non-profits across the UK. And every car dealership partners with local charities and community projects to make a difference. To my mind, it is no surprise that he is building a highly successful, industry-leading business. He is leading with soul. And people notice. Gradually, over time, word gets around. This becomes known as a good place to work. Good people apply there. And the word gets out.

The Kind organizations of the past are still remembered. Thomas Nelson, of my native Edinburgh, is known for the free hot chocolate and employee bowling club and for the social events in the Nelson Hall. Those apprenticeships became like gold dust, passed from father and mother to daughter and son. Similarly, Cadbury, Rowntree, Colman's, Barclays – these principled employers engendered trust and respect. Working for them was, on the whole, something to be proud of; representing them was, for the most part, an honour and a privilege.

People before profit, you see, is not just about your employees; it's also about the impact that organization has on its community. This is no simple task, but it's a vital one.

Start by addressing margin as organizational kindness. Make some and leave some:

- *Create margin:* Where your organization sees people as human beings who have full and complex lives, not just as producers or product, it starts a conversation about expectation and health. Have that conversation, it will include such topics as holiday entitlement, weekend and evening working, health provision and workload. There are no easy answers, but these are Kind discussions.
- *Leave margin:* You don't need to wring every dollar or pound out of every deal; it's hard to be Kind if you insist on doing so. Equally you might not need to beat all your competitors all the time, it might serve you better to collaborate sometimes. If your business or charity or church is one that only takes from the community, or is only transactional in its dealings, where is the kindness in that? And indeed, where is the future goodwill?

THE LAW OF INDIRECT EFFORT

Brian Tracey's book *Maximum Achievement* highlights a concept he calls 'The Law of Indirect Effort.'[108] His hypothesis is that in relationships, the best way to attain whatever it is we seek is indirectly. If you want someone to respect you, you must start by respecting them. If you would like people to be interested in you, you need to begin by being interested in them. In other words, the Golden Rule. Do unto others as you would have them do unto you. It really works.

If you desire personal happiness, think about creating an environment in your home and at your workplace that is bent on pursuing the greatest possible good for *everyone else* and then watch what happens for them and you.

> For success, like happiness, cannot be pursued; it must ensue, and it only does so as the unintended side-effect of one's personal dedication to a cause greater than oneself as the by-product of one's surrender to a person other than oneself.[109]
>
> VICTOR FRANKL, *MAN'S SEARCH FOR MEANING*

And what is true in the science of human relationships is also true in so many other areas of life. If you want a healthy profit for your organization – concentrate on building a healthy culture in your teams. HIHO. If you want performance – invest in relationships.

When, in an essay for the *New York Times* in 1970, Milton Friedman asserted that the one social responsibility of a business is to increase its profits, he was making a powerful point.[110] He was, at one and the same time, totally right and absolutely wrong. If a business fails to make profit it will ultimately fail to exist. But, if a business makes its focus profit before people (or product or planet), it will not make a sustainable profit and will cease to exist.

108 Brian Tracey, *Maximum Achievement* (HarperCollins, 1998), p15.
109 Viktor E. Frankl, *Man's Search for Meaning.* 4th ed. (Beacon Press, 1992), p84.
110 Milton Friedman, 'The Social Responsibility of Business is to Increase Its Profits' in *New York Times* (13 September 1970), p13.

The leader who leads from the Table, who leads with kindness, has a more rounded perspective. They:

- See a bigger picture
- Have a longer plan
- Think a layer deeper

They lead beyond themselves and their self-interest. They choose with a view to those beyond their tenure or even their lifetime. They look below the superficial, think deeper than the urgent and decide for the important.

Never has this point needed to be understood more. If you want profit – invest in people. To invest in people you must build teams. To build teams you must practise the art of the Kind.

MAKE THE TABLE SAFE

Consider this matrix.[111] In fact, study it.

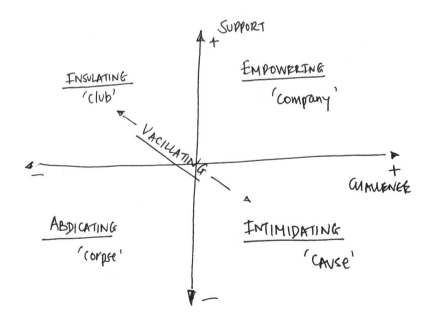

111 I have expanded upon the matrix offered by Ian Day and John Blakey: Ian Day and John Blakey, *Challenging Coaching*. 2nd ed. (Sage, 2012), p17.

Kind Leaders, like good parents and great coaches, know how to calibrate support and challenge. These leaders create an environment of safety *and* stretch. Their teams know that ideas will be heard and not rejected out of hand, and that, at the same time, they will be personally challenged to reach their full potential.

What's your natural leadership style?

Insulating: High support and super safe but offering no real challenge. The team will enjoy being around but will never be as purposeful or productive as they might be. They are likely to have a predisposition towards lethargy, stagnation and boredom. Unattended, the culture becomes entitled, self-serving and stifling and the team becomes a CLUB.

Intimidating: Highly demanding and offering no true support.
The team is likely to know why they are there and what they need to achieve, but they won't like being there. Cynicism, churn and burnout is consciously just around the corner. Unexposed, this culture becomes bullish, driven, unappreciative and toxic. The organization is faced with constant resignations and rehires. The team feels more like a CAUSE.

Vacillating: Inconsistent in approach, offering the worst of support and challenge.
A desire on the part of the leader to protect and support, and to avoid conflict at all costs, leads to a superficial peace and unsatisfactory performance. When patience is exhausted a flipping ensues, and the insulator becomes an intimidator. The result is the antithesis of safe – unsafe, a leadership style that is no longer dependable. In extreme frustration, almost all insulators snap and undermine themselves. The team is, often, CONFUSED.

Abdicating: Absence of or denial of leadership of any kind.
The team is offered no support and no challenge. They operate as individuals with little or no purpose, clarity or development. Over

time, these teams die off or are cut off. Your team has gone and all you are left with is a CORPSE.

Empowering: A healthy team environment of inclusion and expansion. The team culture is such that individuals feel safe, so they can be stretched well. Leaders are perpetually calibrating support and challenge and raising other leaders in this way of relational influence. This zone is the home of all high-performing teams and the territory of all empowering leaders. Consistency reigns here. The team is a COMPANY.

Who are you as a leader?

Where does your team tend to hang out?

What is the journey that must be made?

SOME JOURNEYS CANNOT BE MADE DIRECTLY

Take two teams.

Team A finds itself in a culture of high support and low challenge led by Angela, a natural insulator, with an occasional tendency to snap. The journey that the team wants to take is the fast and direct road to empowerment. That journey, unfortunately, is just not possible. Angela is promoted and her replacement has considerable expectations and introduces more challenge. The team struggles through a maze of new responsibilities where it appears that all support has been lost. It hasn't, but in this unfamiliar world of high challenge support feels absent.

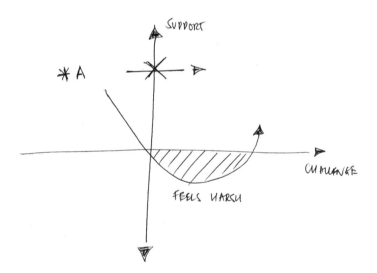

Team B has the opposite starting point: one of high challenge and low support; they are experiencing the cynicism, churn and burn under intimidating leadership, and the culture is driven, bullish and toxic. They too want to move towards empowerment, but when a new CEO with a more supportive, orderly management style takes over, it feels like challenge has lessened. It hasn't, but the team loses momentum and they meander through an unproductive valley for a time.

For both teams, it will take time for truth to be experienced and the land to be reached. And during that time, leaders will emerge and grow. Soul Leaders not only lead people to this cultural space of empowerment; they are also made on the journey.

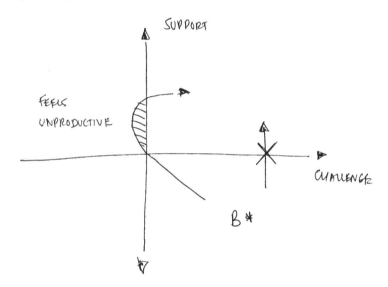

The Kind leader leads his or her people towards a safe place where they might attempt unsafe things – dangerous things, risky things, exciting things, profitable things. At the same time, they are building a culture of team that models and catalyzes health.

START WITH SAFE

Starting with safe is what will grow your team. It's true for parenting – your family feeling safe is the best platform for your children becoming all they might be. It's true for your team as well as your larger organization; maximum contribution flows from maximum belonging.

Abraham Maslow had it right when he developed his hierarchy of human needs.[112]

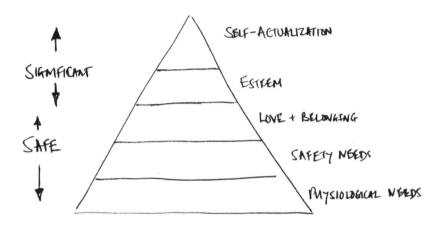

He realized that before you get concerned about self-actualization (purpose/meaning/fulfilment), you must pay attention to survival, security and belonging. In other words, safety must precede significance. If you don't have safety, you cannot have thriving. The best part of a century later that was precisely the outcome of Google's 'Project Aristotle'.[113]

In 2012, Google commissioned an exhaustive survey into the productivity of its numerous teams. After a year of research into over 180 teams, 'Project Aristotle' found that the most important

112 Abraham Maslow, 'A Theory of Human Motivation' in *Psychological Review* 50.4 (1943), pp370–396.
113 Charles Duhigg, 'What Google Learned From Its Quest to Build the Perfect Team', *The New York Times,* 25 February 2016, nytimes.com (accessed 20 August 2023).

determining factor in high performing teams wasn't IQ, experience level or educational pedigree, but something a bit more surprising: 'psychological safety.' Other high-ranking traits were dependability, structure and clarity, meaning and impact, but the quality that eclipsed them all was safety. What Google discovered was that a level of emotional intelligence and empathetic vulnerability had a crucial impact on productivity, retention and success. When people feel safe, seen and heard, they will contribute freely and bring their creative best.

Amy Edmondson, Novartis Professor of Leadership and Management at Harvard Business School, has popularized the term 'psychological safety' and describes it as 'a belief that neither the formal nor informal consequences of interpersonal risks, like asking for help or admitting failure, will be punitive.'[114] She goes on to say, and Google proved, that teams who made mistakes were actually more successful than others. Safe teams embrace trust and create space for radical innovation, pushing organizations forward. These teams also act as breakwaters to seriously dangerous practice, as they learned to speak truth with freedom.

Does every member of your team experience safety in the team? Are all members of your team seen? Heard? Honoured? Would *they* say they were? Do you see them? Hear them? You know their names, but do you hear their dreams? Do you know their fears? Do you know them?

You might have thought it strange that we used the word 'company' to describe a team that is empowered; those words are not always found in the same sentence! Yet technically, that's what a true company feels: empowered.

The etymology of the word 'company' is fascinating. From the Latin 'bread fellow,' the coming together of two words: '*com*',

114 Amy C. Edmondson, *The Fearless Organization: Creating Psychological Safety in the Workplace for Learning, Innovation, and Growth* (John Wiley & Sons, 2018), p15.

meaning 'with' or 'together', and '*panis*', meaning 'bread'. The word in origin describes how merchants would gather to trade, to tell stories and eat together.

Great companies are built and run by 'bread fellows'; those who curate supportive and stretching environments, those who carry and embody safety. As I work with these companies of various sizes and in almost every discipline it is evident that the key quality of these 'bread fellows' is trust. They trust and they are trusted.

SAFETY TRAVELS AT THE SPEED OF TRUST

In the book *The Trusted Advisor*,[115] by David H Maister, Charles H Green and Robert M Galford, it's argued that trust in a team or organization has certain characteristics and isn't as binary as we often choose to make it. It's not 'I trust you' or 'I don't trust you'. It might be more 'I trust you for some things and not for others'; or even more, 'I'm growing in trust for you in these areas and finding it difficult to trust you in these.'

Trust is such a vital commodity for high performance in a team that finding a way to understand and even measure this is a gamechanger. And you must find it, measure it. If you are to have 'bread fellows' or be a 'pack', if you are to lead with kindness for relationships, you must travel at the speed of trust, as does safety.

Below is *The Trusted Advisor* equation:

$$Trust = \frac{Credibility + Reliability + Intimacy}{Self\text{-}Orientation}$$

115 David H. Maister, Charles H. Green, and Robert M. Galford, *The Trusted Advisor: 20th Anniversary Edition* (Free Press, 2021).

In my company we borrow heavily from this, but our equation reads:

$$Trust = \frac{Credible + Dependable + Relatable}{Selfish}$$

Credible: Can I trust your competence? Do you have the abilities, experiences and tools to do what we need? Of course, not all credibility is equal. The ability of the surgeon to cut into my knee is a different credible to the talent of my barber to cut into my hair. Equally, I don't want either doing the other's job!

Dependable: Will you deliver on your promise? Do you do what you say you will do when you say you will do it? Will you have my back when I need you to?

Relatable: Are you knowable, open and vulnerable to the point that it is clear to others that they are dealing with a 'straight shooter'? And, are you seeking to build relational bridges by a deep knowing of others in the team?

Selfish: Are you, at heart, only in it for yourself, concerned to protect, promote and prioritize your ends? It all rises or comes crashing down right here.

$$T = \frac{C + D + R}{S}$$

Three thoughts become immediately apparent for me:
1. All gains above the line are undermined by dysfunction below the line. *The Trusted Advisor* points out that the top line qualities

act as the numerator and the lower line as the denominator. Overt selfishness brings into question the significance of credibility, dependability or relationality. 'Is my experience of being served, honoured and brought into a circle of trust only part of a larger game that will result primarily in benefit to the instigator?'

2. Becoming more relatable might just be the doorway to deep trust. The transparency required to build true relationships and show up with vulnerability is in the same muscle grouping as the generosity required to give of myself on behalf of others, for others, preferring others. If you learn to use one you can learn to employ the other. It is Kind at the core to allow yourself to be fully known, as it is kindness personified to prefer another human being over and above your best interest.

3. Showing up to give as opposed to showing up to get is, in truth, the key thought here. I give my gifts, my energy and myself to my team and this task. This is Kind; kindness in action.

Dr Gareth Clegg is one of the smartest people I know. Gareth works as a consultant in the Accident & Emergency department of a major city hospital; he is also a research professor at one of the oldest universities in the world and the associate director of the Scottish Ambulance Service. His whole career has been given over to saving lives and working out how to help other people do the same. Indeed, a few years ago, Gareth pioneered the organization Save a Life for Scotland – a movement committed to the education and then equipping of a nation to provide a first class 'first responder' service for the nation. It literally saves lives.

This commitment finds its expression in a forensic obsession with cardiac arrests. In a recent interview, he discussed the controversial practice of placing cameras on the uniforms of heart attack first responders. He wanted to achieve two results: firstly, to offer a live conversation between the first responder and fellow experts back in the hospital, widening the circle of wisdom and militating against simple mistakes; secondly, he wanted to analyze practice so everyone could improve. The camera was crucial!

Not surprisingly, in a world of blame and litigation, Gareth had to contend with suspicion and fear, 'What will the footage be used for?' 'Where will the films go?' 'What happens if I make a mistake?' 'Will I be responsible and then culpable in the event of death?' Trust here is everything, the difference between life and death.

In the city where he works and with the team that he has grown, he's held in high esteem and deeply trusted. Consequently, the fear that could have been experienced was overridden and the concerns about reprisals dissipated. The cameras were welcomed, the opportunities for learning and support embraced, and the trials were an overwhelming success. Lives were saved because trust accessed through relationship overcame fear.

In a fascinating contrast, despite the unprecedented success of this experiment on his home patch, when the remote camera was offered to other regions in which Dr Clegg and the team were not known, and therefore not wholly trusted, the project was treated with greater suspicion and ultimately rejected. Lives that might have been saved, have not been.

If trust is the gamechanger, relationship is the gatekeeper. It changes teams, and, in some instances, can even save lives. If relationship is the gatekeeper, the gate it opens is to a path called selflessness. Any agency I have in me to orientate to self must be resisted to gain and keep trust. That is worth repeating, possibly aloud.

Any agency in me that orientates towards self must be resisted to gain and keep trust.

The opposite spirit of 'selfish' might be 'serve others.' The antidote to selfish might be to serve more. I'm sure that cuts across many popular self-improvement mantras – but there it is anyway: if you want to be trusted, you have to be a giver, not a grabber.

Remember Abraham Maslow and his hierarchy? Just after he died, a journal was found which revealed his doubts about his original model.[116] He confessed an 'uneasiness' about self-actualization sitting at the pinnacle of life. He even considered writing a critique of his own work, and he was on his way to articulating that a self-focused actualization should sit lower than a higher ideal of self-transcendence when he died. The psychological world was left without a fully formed rework. Interestingly, even after his journals were found and published, his peers, disciples and critics did not amend his model, likely fearing this additional tier felt too spiritual – too 'soulish'. And yet it must be true that a focus on others over self is the pinnacle of human achievement. Isn't that what we venerate, reward and honour in our sagas and legends? And most value in our leaders?

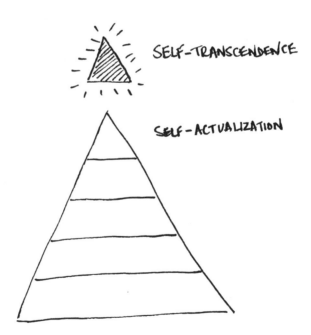

116 Abraham H. Maslow, *The Farther Reaches of Human Nature* (Arkana, 1971).

I think he was, in the final analysis, right, and we are continually less right as we peddle his original model without these later amendments. There is something greater than personal fulfilment – we might call it societal contribution, or just being Kind.

I am fascinated by the potential of the trust that might be gained and kept if, in every arena of my life (team, organization, clients, community), those who experienced me, truly had reason to believe I was in it for them as much as myself.

How can I serve others with kindness? I am exercised by these questions:

How do others experience themselves when I am in the room?
Do they feel seen, heard, involved, honoured?
Who could I become, that this might be true?
Who could we become, that this might be reality?
What could we do, that this might be the result?

You are absolutely the project, but you are certainly not the point of the project. They are.

CHANGE AGENTS

The Greek philosopher Heraclitus of Ephesus supposedly coined the saying, 'Change is the only constant in life.'[117]

Change is going to happen, to you and around you. It can also happen through you, because of you and benefit those who look to you. For the best leaders are change agents, leaders who have learned to navigate this constant in such a way that they are no longer victims of it or surprised by it but masters and experts, bringing 'fixing' because of it.

Being Kind is the only way this works.

I sometimes find myself daydreaming about going back in time

---

117 Writings from both Plato and Marcus Aurelius attribute this phrase to Heraclitus.

and being able to tutor my young leadership self. That leadership self was often confident, but hadn't fully worked out how to lead people well. Chief among the modules I would teach myself would be entitled 'the art of the Kind'; how to do change well would be foundational to that teaching.

You see, while an agreement to being Brave carries within it much of what is needed to bring about change, unless it is aligned with being Kind, it runs the risk of being implemented poorly.

You will have seen this play out in the building moves, the management buyouts, the corporate rebrands, the cabinet reshuffles or even just the office redesign, the new org chart or the five-year vision. You will have likely also observed that organizations who do change badly consequently become change resistant and are unlikely to enter their future well. Or not have one at all. The fallout from toxic or just clumsy processes catastrophizes change and denudes it of its power to offer better opportunities.

The power of Kind played out in a clear plan, and an empathetic pace to bring about healthy transformation and offer an alternative to this oft played out scenario is remarkable.

Borrowing from organizational and psychological models (the Kubler-Ross Change Curve,[118] Bridges' Transitional Model,[119] Virginia Satir's Change Model,[120] and Neish's Change Loop[121]), we often map out a change journey for our clients, as we encourage healthy change as a normative process.

Let me show you:

Disruption – Disorientation – Acceptance – Adoption

118 Elizabeth Kubler-Ross, *On Death and Dying* (Macmillan, 1969).
119 William Bridges, *Transitions: Making Sense of Life's Changes* (Addison-Wesley, 1980).
120 Virginia Satir, *The Satir Model: Family Therapy and Beyond* (Science and Behavior Books, 1991).
121 Developed by David Neish, a change management consultant.

- *Disruption:* The initiation of change usually occurs through some experience of disruption – a death, a firing, a pandemic or just a different direction.

- *Disorientation:* Disruption often leads to a mild disorientation, or on other occasions, a 'hot mess'. The old order of things has been removed or altered and there is insecurity. Which way is up or down? What is right or wrong?

- *Acceptance:* As disorder is recognized and time passes, a calming occurs, usually with a growing acceptance of the end of the 'old' way and a lessening of concern about the 'new' thing. Life may never return to its original shape, but the feelings surrounding the chaos begin to lose their power.

- *Adoption:* When this process is undertaken well, it creates the conditions for sensible conversations about embracing a new way of being that might be even better than the old.

Being Kind in this process is largely a paying of attention to the internal transitions that *must* be made in the tumult of the external changes that *are* being made and carrying hope carefully, particularly when it seems absent.

That hope has different personae and identities at every stage in this process.

WHAT DOES HOPE LOOK LIKE?

Hope looks like honesty in disruption

To name the loss and pain is Kind. Before you can venture toward acceptance, acknowledge what will be missed. Don't deny it. You must articulate the ending of what was for any new beginning to take hold. It's almost impossible to grasp what is while attempting to hold onto what's behind. Above all, you must resist the temptation to rebrand pain, or spin loss as gain. Call it what it is, and you will engender trust for the next step on the change trip.

Hope looks like empathy in disorientation

Your people will have to face fear and you will have to walk through that fear with them. There is no way to circumvent the anxiety that they will feel, and that you will too. It is present in almost all forms of change.

And real hope comes in two forms: your presence and learned resilience.

- *Presence:* They need you to be with them, alongside them, a companion on the Road, not at arm's length, removed from the volatility or uncertainty. They need to hear believable stories about how you are experiencing the change and see that you are willing to iterate the process to suit everyone. They will benefit from proximity to your honesty, your stability, your patience and perseverance; your ability to walk through the changes you are expecting of them.

  Napoleon understood this really well, in truth it might have been the secret of his rise to power.[122] He was a 'hands on', alongside, present leader. He had risen through the ranks, so he knew what it was like to be a common soldier. When finally in command, he resisted the temptation to set himself apart as many of his counterparts did. Instead, in the field, he would walk among the tents, stopping and sitting by the fires, talking and joking with his men. The result was that they would follow him anywhere, irrespective of the difficultly. Napoleon understood the power of his presence, and his participation in leading his men to the type of change that would ultimately impact a continent. He was affectionately known as '*Le Petit Caporal*' – initially an insult, then quickly a nickname, for the down-to-earth manner in which he was with his troops. He

122 Andrew Roberts, *Napoleon: A Life* (Penguin Books, 2014).

knew this was the most effective way he could enroll them in change.

As the leader walks and talks with their team through fear, they begin to minimize and then neutralize its nefarious power. This process is known as exposure therapy.[123]

- *Resilience:* If you want to overcome a fear or a paralyzing anxiety, the commonly shared wisdom is that you need to face it. Gradual, repeated exposure to the source of your specific phobia, combined with a reframing of beliefs around the impact of whatever it is you fear, enables patients to defy the restricting responses.

  It works for specific phobias and it works for fear itself. The more we expose ourselves to fear, the more we understand the nature of it and our default responses to it, the greater the possibility of growing because of it.

  Keep walking through it. Gain clearer perspective along the way ('this will pass', 'I can learn in this', 'this is not the end of the story'). It's not just the Brave that face fear head on, it's also the Kind; it's the only way to get to acceptance.

Hope looks like patience in acceptance

The acceptance that is needed cannot be announced by another or borrowed; it must be experienced personally. To get there, your people may need you to slow down! Set a pace that is walkable.

Pause here a moment.

It is usually more important that change is embraced, and that

123 Jonathan S. Abramowitz, Brett J. Deacon, and Stephen P.H. Whiteside, *Exposure Therapy for Anxiety: Principles and Practice*, Second edition (The Guilford Press, 2019).

you take as many people as possible into Adoption, having grown their own 'change muscles,' than that it happens according to your original optimal timeline.

Read that again.

So, moderate other priorities to make space for the activities that are going to help them make the trip. It will cost in time, energy and the pursuit of those other priorities, but this forensic attention to a Kind process, a Kind presence and a Kind pace will reap incredible rewards.

You can't force Adoption because you can't prescribe Acceptance – every time you attempt to do this you undermine your leadership and the change journey. It will come. In its time. Eventually, those you are leading through change will find their own voice saying, 'it's going to be okay.' They will reach a peace. Only then can Adoption be embraced and the change journey completed.

Ironically, any noble attempt to avoid the pain and uncertainty of change by short-cutting the experience of change has the opposite effect. We become risk-averse, fearful of disruption and lose our ability to create, speculate and grow. In doing so we bequeath to our teams, even our families, a fragility that is likely to break them as they are exposed to further, deeper and more wide-reaching change.

On the flip side, if you can be Kind as you lead change, you set your people up for futures full of health and growth. Change, while not always embraced as a friend, will cease to be the pantomime villain of organizations and become rather what it is: the necessary pathway to all good progress.

Kindness is not some sort of weak, nice, non-leadership trait; it's the stuff that all great leaders are made of. It gets the job done. This is not just 'nice,' it's smart, for when you lead kindly, the team around you can be bold and speculative without fear of ridicule or cynicism. When kindness becomes the operating system of your leadership, people begin to appreciate their working environment and give more of themselves. The right people hang around and the best people clamour to join. The organization itself becomes known for its kindness because this quality is highly contagious.

But if being Kind is to be caught, it must first be carried. You need to have it to pass it on.

So, be Kind to yourself. It's not selfish. Kindness, like bravery and truth and curiosity, bleed out of you.

Ask the teams at Google. Or Phil Jackson. Better still, my he-knows-my-name friend Jack. In fact, if you ever meet him, try to get an invitation to his Table.

THE CAVE

THE ROAD

THE TABLE

THE FIRE

CHAPTER 9

THE FIRE:
the pursuit of the Curious

> May every sunrise hold more promise and every sunset hold more peace.

TRADITIONAL IRISH PRAYER

This blessing is, I think, best received in a resonant Irish brogue and with a glass in hand. It will only be appropriated when you understand that you can't live the first part of it without experiencing the last. Evenings that come to peace are followed by days that are promising.

It is, of course, not a new idea. Great thinkers and leaders down the years have modelled this 'pursuit of the curious' by carefully managing their sunsets, practising what we call stoking the Fire.

Benjamin Franklin was one of those leaders; 'What good have I done today?' he would ask himself at the close of each evening. It wrapped up his thinking and became his nightly ritual: 'At night, I examined the day's transactions, my faults and omissions. I made all the necessary corrections for the next day. I never went to sleep without an examination of the day.'[124] He followed the same pattern every sunset with a desire to improve himself daily and live into the promise of the sunrise. It was his way of making sure that he put himself back 'in the circle' the next morning, True, Brave, Kind and Curious. Stoking the Fire is my attempt to do the same, to interrogate the project and stay the course.

---

124 Benjamin Franklin, *The Autobiography of Benjamin Franklin*, Edited by J. A. Leo Lemay (Yale University Press, 1986), p40.

Any experience that remains unprocessed stays unlearned.

Take that in for just a moment, read it again if you want. Any experience that remains unprocessed stays unlearned.

Your Fire might be a wood burner in Norway, licking gnarled softwood logs and kicking out sparking heat. It might not be so much a fire, as a mackerel sunset over the Western isles, one you can't help but hike out to gaze on. Your Fire might be a floor cushion under a Velux window from which you can glimpse the rooftops, powerlines and chimney stacks of your quietening city, the kids asleep, the chores all done, a moment to remember yourself and gather your day. Whatever your Fire is, it must be a close and a review.

Whatever your context, whatever your rhythm, you must try to reflect. Whether you journal in ink on paper or type single-fingered on a keyboard, you must try to reflect and review. Or you will not learn and grow.

Me? I just happen to love a fire.

We built a pit on the flat edge of the steep hill that stands watch over the oxbow stream on the farthest reaches of our property. We had help, but together we cleared the ground, dug the hole, hauled the logs, lifted the stones and created the most perfect circle for reflection. It cost nothing but time, sweat and a couple of splinters. There are cozier, costlier and more comfortable spaces at our home, but perhaps none more special than this.

When we gather around that fire ring, I'm in charge.

I measure the harvested beech for moisture, split the wood, stack the pile, lay the kindling and light the twigs with the silver pipe lighter that is almost never used for its designed purpose. I revere this task more than any other and I'm not sharing – the Fire is my domain.

There is something primal and magnetic about that fire. A long, light summer night poking the embers, ducking the sparks and pondering subjects, somehow made more accessible by their softening glow.

Niki and I have hosted many gatherings at our house in the Scottish hills. We have taught principles, coached and provoked possibilities, but invariably, it's the fireside times that have catalyzed the greatest breakthroughs and made a way for the realization of visions and futures.

Laughter-filled family celebrations, fond memories and fresh hope, New Year's Eve gatherings with dreams and resolutions, retreats closed out with agreements sealed in the flames all linger long in the mind. No less sacred are the winter's evenings sitting around log-burners, sipping single malts, reflecting with friends on the day spent and those to come.

It's the focus that the Fire offers; it's not the Fire itself, it's what the Fire makes possible. It's the confession of failures, the garnering learnings, the speaking of hope and the blessing of futures that makes it a 'thin place'.

The Fire is the pursuit of the Curious.

And so, it has become the close of many of my days. Alone, with mildly acrid woodsmoke and full thoughts for company. Time spent raking over the ashes of encounters, conversations and challenges have not just made me a better leader, but, I like to believe, also a better person. The Fire, in this regard, serves as both classroom and confessional. It is a safe place to do dangerous reflection, a clearing ground for the thoughts and learnings that are the very materials from which soul growth happens.

If you don't stoke the Fire, it will be hard for you to lead from this deeper place.

You see, unless you make room at the close of the day for this practice, there's a significant probability that its learnings will be lost to you. The Cave, the Road and the Table will then become a 'Groundhog Day' experience, an ever-repeating 24 hours of good intentions, careful refocusing and communal discussion, which, unapplied, go nowhere and make little difference for you. A stress cycle and never a success loop:

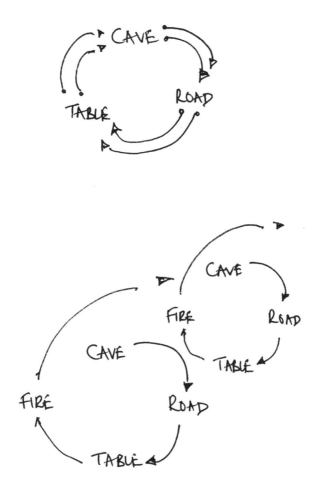

In this pattern, the Fire is catalytic. It's a moment of a reflection that bundles up that day and allows its lessons to become building blocks for a better tomorrow.

Remember, what you focus on today, you give permission to exist tomorrow. So, set aside time to inventory the day to extract the learning from it. Whether you have the opportunity to light a fire, put a match to a candle, or just open a journal, you must process.

As I was writing this book, I engaged in a debate with my publisher about the nature of book reviews. She had come across a comment that any book you do not review in some way or other, you might almost as well not have read! We agreed that the position was overstated; surely some books were meant to be lost in, laughed about and just enjoyed? After reflection and some backtracking, I now, almost, buy into the statement. Because … any experience that remains unprocessed stays unlearned. Right? Unprocessed experiences will likely stay undiscovered and undealt with.

Most simply, the goal of the Fire is to shore up answers to these two questions:

What did I learn today?
How might I act tomorrow?

Ten minutes might be enough. To answer those two pivotal questions by forensically exploring three areas:

- *What do I want to take with me into tomorrow?*
- *Leave behind in today?*
- *Get right in my relationships now?*

Write it down with these headings: TAKE WITH, LEAVE BEHIND and GET RIGHT

I have a notebook on the go constantly. Gnarled leather, thick paper and full of chaotic ponderings, it's at hand to record ideas throughout the day and then to revisit at night. My Fire time is in significant part the sense-making and synthesising of these scribblings. The simple act of journaling is, for me, an attempt to recall and retain the lessons of a life easily wasted. It is the art of capturing moments and their meanings that allows me to appropriate them for my future. Writing enables me to get my soul in order. It's a thought processing tool that makes for better tomorrows.

Examine the good, the bad, the ugly and the downright confusing. Process it to bring it to clarity and get it to simple, to make it useful.

Oliver Wendell Holmes, former Chief Justice of the Supreme Court of the United States of America, once made a distinction between two kinds of simplicity. He called them 'near side' and 'far side' simplicity.[125] His distinction was between the simplicity of lazy thinking, which relied on shallow-mindedness and broad-brush understanding, and far side simplicity, that had passed through the crucible of thought and experience and had been proven.

Many leaders and teams settle for truth that convinces very few: 'It is because it is because it is.' Others live in complex truth, which confuses most and has not been wrestled to the ground in a way that can be lived out or articulated.

Leading from the soul calls for a simplicity on the far side of complexity. A simple leadership fights for clear understanding and wrestles hard ideas to the ground.

Journal to process it all; it's a battle for 'far-side simplicity'. Opening your journal is laying the sticks. Writing in it is lighting the kindling. Learning from it is the Fire.

125 John Paul Lederach, *The Moral Imagination: The Art and Soul of Building Peace* (Oxford University Press, 2005), p33.

TAKE WITH

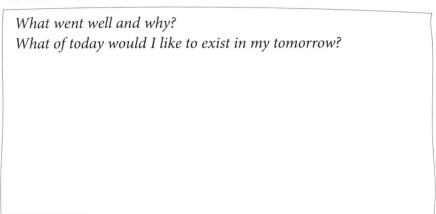

What went well and why?
What of today would I like to exist in my tomorrow?

Where did I win today and why?
What was the change agent in the process?
How can I add that to my leadership tool kit?

What have you learned today about your unique contributions to this life? How can you spend more of your time doing more of the things that align with your yes, your unique contribution? How can you build on the experiences and relationships that appear to have traction right now?

As you examine your day, pay attention to the affirmations given and the ground taken. What prompted them? What were the words said or the goals achieved? How might that territory taken today be secured and built on for other days? This conversation with yourself is deeper than the talk of the Table. It's more than highs and lows – it's a dive into the grows.

The kind of leadership you are seeking is not afraid of questions and conflict; indeed, it welcomes debate and doubt. Growth happens best in a culture of questioning. As in all these things, it starts with you.

So, as you probe further, ask tangible questions about what you experienced and the role you played and how you learned and how that might stay with you:

- *What was it?*
- *Why was it?*
- *How was it?*
- *And, how might I apply it?*

LEAVE BEHIND

What did not go well and why?
What of today needs to remain in today and needs to not be repeated tomorrow? What can I glean from the worst mistakes, the harshest critique or the strongest triggers?

By now you will probably have gathered that I love words; the more 'old school' the sound, the more I love them. I particularly enjoy the word 'glean'. In early English, the word first appears around the fourteenth century and means to gather the scrapings. [126] It is a concept borrowed from early agricultural practice. When fields were being harvested, local villagers were given permission to 'glean' from the edges of the land the crops that hadn't been cut. To redeem well is to 'glean' from the negative experiences of the day the learnings that would otherwise be lost to you. Gleaning flows from a desire to not miss anything of value for the health of your soul.

If I can glean, I can gain. And if I can gain, I can imbue a negative experience with a growth opportunity, even overwrite it with possibility. Of course, if you are to gain growth from a personal defeat, you must have a mature approach to failure.

Two perspectives are vital here:

1. *Failure is an event, not a person.* Failure is not who you are. It is not your identity. And yet. Failure will continue to be a person – YOU – unless you intentionally make it an event – IT.

One way to ensure it's an event is to clarify and apply its lessons. Failure can only grow you if you face it. Don't sugar coat it. Call it a failure, embrace its mess, accept your part in it and then determine to act in other, better ways going forward.

2. *Total failure is rarely fatal, so stop treating it as if it is.* If you can look objectively, even the greatest life crashes offer some learning opportunities. My leadership journey has often proven this.

Failure teaches us lessons. Makes us approachable. Keeps us humble. Enables us to empathize with others. Helps us avoid greater and wider damage in the future. Gives us the unique wisdom that only comes from experience. Use it, for your benefit!

In the acting profession, as they're being trained in theatre craft, budding thespians are often taught to 'use the difficulty'.[127] When they enter the stage and fall over, or attempt to go through a

126 The first published use of the word was in the Oxford English Dictionary in the fourteenth century. It may be Celtic in origin.
127 Robert Cohen, *The Actor's Art and Craft* (McGraw-Hill, 1978), p12.

stage door and it will not open, or are interrupted mid-speech by a mistake from a co-star, 'use the difficulty' – don't stumble over it or fumble it, but use it to enhance the moment. Don't pretend it didn't happen, but add it to the script; riff off it and use it to build rapport with the audience. As it is on the stage, 'use the difficulty' can be employed in life. As you know, leadership is not a smooth road; it's cluttered with persistent difficulty – rocks in the way that can knock you down, block your path or be climbed on to create better vistas. Failure is learning.

This Fire is the making of a moment for you to sit with your failure as much as you bathe in your success. Your True, Brave, Kind, Curious self is forged in the crucible of wins and losses and how they are processed.

GET RIGHT

At the close of the day, find peace. Write the word 'peace' in your journal. This might just be the most important fireside word. By peace I mean a sense of contentment, of rightness, alignment and integrity. It is well with my soul.

What I have seen, repeatedly, is that an inability to move on from a hurt, a mistake or a toxic relationship can so easily become the primary blocker to the growth of a leader. The things you can't forgive in others, yourself, or in your history, are the very things that keep you from True, Brave, Kind and Curious and the fulfilment of your potential.

GET RIGHT (WITH YOURSELF)

For peace to be your experience, freedom must be your context, so get right with yourself!

That freedom – a freedom from assumption, judgment, hurt and loss – is found largely in the practice of forgiving yourself and then others.

Unforgiveness is a prison.

Stop here.

I'm not asking you to engage in some kind of religious process or any kind of strange primal ritual. I'm just encouraging you to free yourself from anything that would disable 'the project'.

Further, what I've discovered, through personal pain, is that my inability to forgive others is inseparably connected to my inability to free myself. In this regard, freeing yourself becomes a generosity to others as much as it is one to your own soul.

So, inventory today and judge it! Put yourself in the dock, cross examine your activities. Did you act in ways inconsistent with your soul?

Was I True today?
Was I Brave today?
Was I Kind today?
Was I Curious today?

Write it down, and as you do so, put on these qualities again. Especially be Kind. The life you lead is not easy, the people you surround yourself with can be difficult, the circumstances around you will often be oppositional, progress may be slow.

The life you desire to lead is harder still.

Being Kind to yourself is not just about feeling good, it's more about growing better, for your soul is easier to access from Kind than it is from harsh. If you can forgive yourself, you can free yourself. In doing so, you are creating the best soil conditions for healthy growth.

SHAME & GUILT

Watch out for the difference between these two powerful drivers. Guilt can be a very helpful emotion; it is triggered by your responsibility for a moment or event that went wrong and makes you feel bad: 'This is what I did.' Guilt, properly worked through, can therefore be a springboard towards growth and development. Make good use of it. Let it do its work.

Conversely, shame is almost always a negative emotion, triggered by an alignment of a mistake or a failure with an identity: 'This is who I am.' Shame is a persona that tends to attach itself to people, and then hangs around limiting futures. It is rarely the doorway to growth and life. If you are to lead from your soul, you must get help to shake off shame.

Shame has many guises. Sometimes it extroverts as performance or escape. It shows itself as a grasping for approval or a running away from it. In other people, it introverts as self-loathing or suppression. It shows itself as a rejection of emotion or a punishing of self – a self-sabotaging.

Always, it stunts soul.

Brené Brown has illuminated in her many books how vulnerability,[128] and the ensuing empathy, is an antidote to shame, because once it is articulated and brought to light, it loses its power. I want to take this further; vulnerability and empathy are necessary treatments, but it's only in forgiveness that freedom comes.

I forgive myself for …
Doing … or not doing
Believing in … or disbelieving
Colluding or cowardice

The action you are not proud of, the mistake you made or the pain you cause, is not YOU – it's what YOU did. If that can be faced – you can be freed.

128 These books by Brené Brown include *The Gifts of Imperfection* (Hazelden Publishing, 2010), *Daring Greatly* (Avery, 2012), *Rising Strong* (Random House, 2015), *Braving the Wilderness* (Random House, 2018), *Atlas of the Heart* (Random House, 2021).

Pause here.

> *Where have you attached shame to an event that failed, a role*
> *that didn't work out or a job in which you didn't succeed?*

Name it. Own your part in it. It isn't YOU. It doesn't define you or limit you. It schools you, if you will let it. Forgive yourself and free yourself. If you can't do this, you won't truly be able to forgive anyone else.

GET RIGHT (WITH OTHERS)

Now you can forgive others for ...

The pain they inflicted
The care they neglected
The words they spoke
The actions that impacted

It serves you well – as much as it does them. It might *look* magnanimous. It might *be* expedient. Numerous studies have shown that bitterness and pain emanating from hurts, historical or current, create stress disorders negatively affecting the immune system. These disorders contribute to heightened anxiety, neuroticism and even death.[129]

There is an enormous physical burden to being hurt and disappointed.[130]

That's Karen Swartz MD, Director of the Mood Disorders Adult Consultation Clinic at The Johns Hopkins Hospital. Swartz points to research that indicates changes in heart rate, blood pressure and immune responses are a direct result of the forgiveness given for a traumatic event or a long-term challenging relationship.[131]

Dr Frederic Luskin, Director of the Stanford University Forgiveness Project[132] (who would have thought such a thing existed?), further asserts that forgiveness in the workplace not only helps the physical and psychological well-being of employees, it helps productivity and profitability, as well.[133] The common practice of forgiveness not only reduces stress and builds trust, the practising of it also grows conflict resolution skills. The resultant

129 These sources all include studies linking bitterness to health problems:
(1) Christopher Peterson, Nansook Park, and Martin Seligman (2000). 'The relationship between bitterness, stress, and health problems' in *Personality and Social Psychology Bulletin*, volume 26 (issue 3), p322–331. (2) Ronald Glaser, Janice Kiecolt-Glaser, and Ronald W. Malarkey (1999), 'Bitterness, hostility, and cardiovascular reactivity' in *Psychosomatic Medicine*, volume 61 (issue 1), p123–129. (3) Michael J. Scheier, Carol C. Carver, and Michael F. Bridges (1994), 'The association between anger, hostility, and blood pressure: A meta-analysis' in *Psychological Bulletin*, volume 116 (issue 1), p63–89.
130 Dr. Swartz has stated this in numerous interviews.
131 Christopher Peterson, Nansook Park, and Martin E. Seligman (2004), 'Forgiveness, heart rate, and blood pressure reactivity' in *Journal of Personality and Social Psychology*, volume 86 (issue 2), p595–603.
132 Frederic Luskin, Ph.D., 'The Art of Forgiveness', *Stanford Medicine,* med. stanford.edu (accessed 21 August 2023).
133 Dr Luskin references many studies in his work, including: Michael McCullough, Everett Worthington Jr., Kimberly Rachal, et al. (1998), 'Forgiveness, forbearance, and constructive responses to interpersonal offense' in *Journal of Social and Clinical Psychology*, volume 17 (issue 1), p1–16.

openness helps teams learn, create and avoid repeated mistakes.[134]

There is a significant sense in which this might be cyclical. If you can't forgive yourself, you will be unlikely to have the agency, legitimacy or power to offer forgiveness to a perpetrator. If you decide not to forgive and free them from obligation, you cannot be truly and materially free yourself. You will remain stuck in what someone else did to you or spoke over you.

You must forgive yourself, so that you get free, so that you can forgive others – so that they have the potential of forgiving themselves, so that they can forgive others. It's not really that complicated, but it might be that big!

The practice of the Fire is, in part, then, a prompt to forgiveness – to free people.

It will serve you well.

As you reflect on the pain of the day, be slow to rush to offence. If you find yourself often offended, you'll need to check your ego. Anger is easy to access.

Be honest about people, but be Kind. You rarely know the full story, the backstory. It is a Kind and powerful practice to attempt a walk in their shoes or to try to see the view from their side.

When facing down what appears to be an attack, or at least obvious opposition, it has helped me to prefer a verdict of 'clumsy' over an assumption of 'malice'. Even if malice might have been the intention, presuming clumsy introduces grace and carves out the space for broader possibility.

Forgive quickly and persistently.

Forgiveness is less a statement and more a resolution. It is an act of the will and often a prolonged process.

134 Everett Worthington Jr., Michael McCullough, Kimberly Rachal, et al. (1998), 'Forgiveness and workplace conflict' in *Personality and Social Psychology Bulletin*, volume 24 (issue 10), pp1144–1157.

I FORGIVE YOU.

I AM FORGIVING YOU.

I WILL FORGIVE YOU.

Any form of forgiveness that doesn't look like a process is probably not forgiveness. It might be some kind of superficial moving on, but it isn't forgiveness. It might be a ceasefire, but it is not peace. And peace is what is going to enable you to lead with freedom.

So:

- *Own the hurt*. Don't deny it. Sit in it long enough to feel it and process it.
- *Articulate the hurt* at the same time as accepting that yours might not be the only story.
- *Become aware* of any feelings of anger and revenge and name them before you ever try to let them go.

This is not a 'once and it's done' activity. But it is a process you must begin if you want to lead unencumbered with the wounds of the past and at peace in the present. Begin a practice of tearing up the I.O.U.s you have written, metaphorically, letting the other go free and getting unstuck yourself.

As you journal you might want to make a plan, to have a conversation, to write a letter or to be less angry. I don't know your pain, but I do know that unprocessed, it cannot heal, and that unhealed wounds cause deeper complications.

Get some help if you think you need it. You must fight for your freedom. Your soul, like mine, needs peace to prosper.

BE AT PEACE

At the end of the day, take a sense check on the day. Inventory it with kindness, suck the learnings out of it with curiosity, and let your soul grow healthy. Write it down in the journal you keep. Now, close the book. Be at peace.

Take with. Leave behind. Get right.

End the day right – right with your True, Brave, Kind and Curious self.

Peace is, of course, not the absence of conflict, but the presence of perspective and calm in the conflict. It is not the fixing of things or even the completing of tasks that allows you to stop and rest, but rather a sense of alignment with soul and a rightness in self, which offers an ability to park the unending 'to-do's of the leadership life to be progressed in a future still to come. And to rest.

So, glean. Leave behind the failings and the misgivings. But take hold of the learnings. Get right with yourself and others. Now close your journal.

And sleep freely.

The practice of the Fire is the pursuit of the Curious.

CHAPTER 10

CURIOUS:
by the Fire

We keep moving forward, opening new doors and doing new things, because we're curious and curiosity keeps leading us down new paths.[135]

WALT DISNEY

The important thing is not to stop questioning. Curiosity has its own reason for existence. One cannot help but be in awe when he contemplates the mysteries of eternity, of life, of the marvellous structure of reality. It is enough if one tries merely to comprehend a little of this mystery each day.[136]

ALBERT EINSTEIN

'We made a runway out of a river.'[137] The words of Captain Chelsey 'Sully' Sullenberger on the heroic effort that he, co-pilot Jeff Skiles and the crew of US Airways flight 1549 made as they emergency-landed a passenger aircraft on the only available, unpopulated geography: the Hudson River in New York City. The remarkable story is one of great poise and courage, and a study in curiosity.

When asked how he was able to stay calm and act decisively under such stress, Sully talks about the more than 20,000 hours of flying time he had logged, and the same for co-pilot Skiles. When pushed further, he talks about how he had approached each of those hours: with continuous, intentional learning.

135 Published in the ending credits of the 2007 animated Disney film *Meet the Robinsons.*
136 Albert Einstein, 'Old Man's Advice to Youth: "Never Lose a Holy Curiosity."' LIFE, May 2, 1955.
137 'Sully' remembers 'Miracle on the Hudson' on 10th anniversary. Good Morning America, ABC News, 15 January 2023.

If you've ever heard Sully speak, you would hear lines like: 'One of the things I teach my children is that I have always invested in myself, and I have never stopped learning, never stopped growing.' There it is – Curious. 'My mother was a first-grade teacher, so I credit her with this lifelong intellectual curiosity I have, and love of reading and learning.'

He possessed not just 20,000 hours of experience, but 20,000 hours of curious learning. 'I was sure I could do it. I think in many ways, as it turned out, my entire life, up to that moment had been a preparation to handle that particular moment.' A life of continuous improvement. A life lived curiously.

THE KAIZEN WAY

Curiosity is central to the success of the Toyota Motor Corporation. The story of Toyota and 'The Toyota Way' is rooted in a company-wide discipline of curiosity, born of the philosophy embraced by Sakichi Toyoda, as he established the 'Toyoda Automatic Loom Works' in the late nineteenth century, and then by generations of the Toyoda family, as they became what is now the largest automobile manufacturer on the planet.[138] The core of this philosophy is *Kaizen,* or continual improvement. Its genesis is the philosophy of '*Genchi Genbutsu,*' Japanese for 'Go and see,' which is literally 'real location, real thing,' and means look hard, detail matters, waste is important. Pace the production floor, walk the garages, pay attention to everything.

The process is this:

- *Go and See:* It is critical to interrogate the initial challenge or problem. This is a non-superficial looking; study what you see deeply.
- *Ask Why?* Ask again … and again. You need to not just know, but to understand if you want to grow.

138 Jeffrey K. Liker, *The Toyota Way: 14 Management Principles from the World's Greatest Manufacturer* (McGraw-Hill, 2004).

- *Marginally Improve:* Take baby steps, but get better all the time.
- *Never Arrive:* Every day is a school day.

Toyota's articulation has far greater detail, but even this simplistic summary, if applied vigorously and humbly, would transform much of what passes for leadership in the corporate world today.

Sir David Brailsford sought to address the radical underperformance of British cycling with something akin to this approach when he became the Team Sky performance director in 2003.[139] His *Kaizen* methodology became known as 'the aggregation of marginal gains'. Brailsford said, 'The whole principle came from the idea that if you broke down everything you could think of that goes into riding a bike, and improve it by 1%, you will get a significant increase when you put them all together.'

Brailsford's 1% plan took him beyond the bike, to the food consumed and the way the riders washed their hands to avoid sickness, to how they rested and slept best. Brailsford had his support crew transport Bradley Wiggins' bed for at least two months, as he rode in and won the Tour de France and then took gold at the London Olympics. He believed there was little that couldn't be improved.

Driven by curiosity, a team that had only won one Olympic gold medal since 1908 and had been perennial underachievers, started to win everything. Under this regime, at the 2008 Olympics in Beijing, the team won 60% of the gold medals available, and under Brailsford's leadership of Team Sky Racing, British riders won six Tour de France titles.

Author James Clear, writing about Brailsford in *Atomic Habits*, reminds the reader that although 1% does not appear a huge margin, if you get 1% better each day at any particular thing, by the end of a year, you'll be 37x better.[140]

---

139 Richard Moore, *Mastermind: How Dave Brailsford Reinvented the Wheel* (Yellow Jersey Press, 2014).
140 James Clear, *Atomic Habits: An Easy & Proven Way to Build Good Habits & Break Bad Ones* (Penguin Random House, 2018), p47.

Imagine being 37x fitter, 37x better as a public communicator, 37x better at reading people. And helping them. Imagine being 37x better at leading your team. The process is, of course, more than curiosity, but it starts there.

Curiosity is the last in our list of qualities and agreements, and yet it is not least in importance. Curiosity is the engine that keeps True authentic, Brave courageous, and Kind connected. In the absence of curiosity, the soul of your leadership grows weak and wanes. This agreement is an agreement to growth and teachability. Curiosity is the pursuit of the wise, and when done continually, its fruit is wisdom.

DO HARD THINGS!

'You can't teach an old dog new tricks!' I was told this repeatedly by people who were stuck. Stuck in comfort zones. Stuck in ways of thinking that reduced their potential. Stuck in ways of behaving that was damaging their relationships. It sounds like a reasonable assertion and yet it's not true. Turns out, you can. With dogs and tricks and humans and thoughts.

Learning these new tricks and growing in new thinking is, in part, the pursuit of the Curious. It starts with a recovery of wonder and a predisposition to possibility, it continues as a passion for learning, growth and wisdom that is entirely possible throughout your life.

Modern neuroscience has proven our brains are more malleable than we would ever have imagined. Daniel Coyle, in his book *The Talent Code*,[141] speaks of his work on 'deep practice' and shows how our brain's plasticity can – through intentionality – form new neural connections, the more we do something and the more we learn, the thicker and stronger those connections become and the more we grow.

---

141 Daniel Coyle, *The Talent Code: Greatness Isn't Born. It's Grown. Here's How* (Bantam, 2009), p23.

He says, 'Deep practice feels a bit like exploring a dark and unfamiliar room. You start slowly, you bump into furniture, stop, think, and start again. Slowly and painfully, you explore the space over and over, attending to errors, extending your reach into the room a bit farther each time, building a mental map until you can move through it quickly and intuitively.'[142] Doing hard things and completing hard things creates these neural superhighways which are not only routes to excellence in our chosen arenas but learned responses that make breakthroughs in other hard things likely. Discipline that results in habit and then lifestyle in one area of your life comes with the promise and probability of the same in others. If we can practise curiosity for long enough and hard enough, *and keep doing so*, we can rewire the brain, retain wonder and grow wiser. The problem we might have is the comfort we so enjoy.

LIMINALITY

Over the past fifty years, psychologists have been rediscovering and reinterpreting a concept known as *liminal space,* a construct first written about by Arnold van Gennep in 1909[143] and developed further by anthropologist Victor Turner in his 1967 work *The Forest of Symbols.*[144]

The phrase has its roots in the Latin word *limin*, meaning threshold, and describes the interspace between two secure realties – a past that is set and a future that will be lived into, but has not yet emerged. It's the space between what was and what will be. Like the hallway in your house or the corridor in your office building, it's generally not a place for lingering, relaxing or entertaining. You don't put your most comfortable furniture in the hall!

142 Coyle, *The Talent Code: Greatness Isn't Born. It's Grown. Here's How*, p80.
143 Arnold van Gennep, Rites de Passage. Translated by Monika B. Vizedom and Gabrielle L. Caffee (University of Chicago Press, 1960).
144 Victor Turner, *The Forest of Symbols: Aspects of Ndembu Ritual* (Cornell University Press, 1970), pp104–111.

Liminal space is essentially an off-balance moment, a space of natural uncertainty. It carries a chaotic quality, and also the seeds of creative possibility. Every dance starts off balance. Every adventure is launched with a gulp of courage and a leap of faith. Every masterpiece is created in the movement from the unknown to the known. It is the space that gets you to every other space. It's the space where you can choose to do things differently and set a new course.

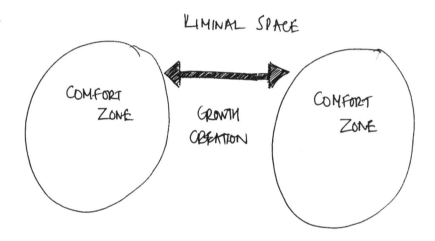

Richard Rohr describes this threshold as the space 'where the old world is able to fall apart, and a bigger world is revealed.'[145]

This space is the habitat of the curious, the space with the greatest potential to change you; leaders who step willingly into it grow as they stretch into all that is possible.

You can't grow in a comfort zone, you grow in 'liminal space', a 'discomfort zone'. Almost all new learning and opportunities, all 'new tricks' and fresh thinking are discovered here, so you have to find it, you need to put yourself in it. I recognize that what we are discussing here is

145 Richard Rohr, 'The Threshold of Transformation' in *The Universal Christ* (Convergent Books, 2019), pp10–15.

challenging; comfort has a very understandable magnetic appeal. There are strong reasons why we are predisposed to automate our lives and to find 'shortcuts' for hard things. There is some wisdom in encouraging young people to 'settle down' and ourselves to 'settle for' the life that is simplest to lead or achieve. The comfort that we experience as we live this way is undoubtedly rewarding and then remarkably limiting, it might even be the suffocation of Soul Leadership. The only treatment I know to break its gravitational pull is to intentionally make friends with discomfort, aggressively shake it up, regularly change it up, open your mind to fresh thoughts and your life to new activities.

To move forward you might need to go back.

WONDER-LOST

Only leaders who make room to dream will be able to do what they dream of. There was a time when I played with sand, modelled with clay, drew outside the lines, had imaginary friends, and believed I was Superman and could probably fly. 'How hard can it be?' was the mantra. I never worried about the worst-case scenario. I had no health and safety concerns and I dressed to be noticed.

Then I grew up. I rejected all notion of flight. One too many bloody knees helped. I started to reason according to the adult world. I traded dreaming for circumspection, observing that leadership seemed ringfenced for those especially good at mitigating risk. The quality that shrunk in me was wonder.

Children carry it well, perhaps naturally. They tend to show up at life wide-eyed. They have not learned yet to be anxious, assume angles, understand the benefit of contorting themselves for each situation. They just show up – open. Most children carry 'why?' well, too.

'Why are we stopping at the lights?'
Because the other cars are going to come across.
'Why don't we just go?'

Because we'll crash.
'Why will we crash?'
Because if we go, they won't be able to stop, and we will collide
und people will get hurt.
'Why?'
Because there are physical laws in the universe, about
momentum and mass and … ahhhh … it is, because I say it is!

Curiosity is how they will know and grow.

Something – someone – somehow – stole our wonder. Life has a habit of doing that to us, have you noticed? We get let down, are disappointed and feel betrayed. We realize that there are consequences to actions, as our pre-frontal cortex starts to develop, and we learn to avoid risk. It is a completely understandable process, and it steals from us some of the potential that is in us. I think that the problem might be that most adult leaders just stop asking 'Why?' as often. We quit wondering. And we end up wondering why we have stopped growing.

The curious wonder, they make space to ask questions, then ask more – and they listen for responses, curate conversations and stay open and agile as long as it is possible before deciding and judging. It makes them great leaders.

WONDERFUL WISDOM

As you rethink wonder in your life, be careful not to sabotage wisdom in its wake. Embrace childlike wonder, but reject childish wisdom.

There is, of course, a place for quick and decisive binary thinking. A time for up and not down, a time for fast and not slow. You don't want your surgeon or your airline pilot in the moment of action to be nuanced in their decision-making, but equally dangerous and destructive for healthy leadership is a binary obsession. It is, for the most part, the stuff of immaturity.

Addiction to 'binary' originates in childhood. We think:

'If there is a winner, there must be a loser.'
'For me to succeed, you have to fail.'
'If one thing is true, the other must be false.'
'If you get your way, I can't have mine.'

I have often seen this limiting thinking continuing well into adulthood, in leaders with significant roles. I'm sure you have observed and experienced the fallout from a desire to oversimplify complex decisions, nuanced conversations, or multi-layered situations. Equally I'm sure you have been party to simplistic categorization, 'they all … ', 'that type … '.

A common psychological game is called 'splitting'[146] – in defence of our ego, we split people. We present them as either 'all good' or 'all bad', depending on how that descriptor would best serve or position us. Not only is this just not true, it is also deeply damaging both to the object of the 'splitting' and you as you practise it.

The truth is that 'binary' thinking is mostly damaging to curiosity, wonder and creativity. It shuts down possibility well before it needs to. There are, often, multiple truths at play and numerous ways to be Brave, Kind or even Curious.

Oversimplification risks missing out on creativity that can only be uncovered in the tension of the wrestle between truths, and leaves us less challengeable, less teachable and less soulful.

The pursuit of the curious is a friendship with paradox, and an ease in the midst of dualism, childlike but not childish. Keep wondering 'Why?' as long and as often as you can, and if possible, don't rush to 'What to do?' about the 'Why' until you must; it will likely lead to a better choice.

146 John R. Gould, Norman M. Prentice, Ricardo C. Ainslie, R.C. (1996). 'The splitting index: construction of a scale measuring the defense mechanism of splitting' in *Journal of Personality Assessment*, volume 66 (issue 2): pp414–430.

5 WHYS

Sakichi Toyoda is generally acknowledged as originating the '5 Why's' technique in the Toyota Motor Company during the evolution of its manufacturing methodologies.[147] This approach to a problem seeks to get to the root of the issue by not settling for superficial responses. Try it. If it has worked for the largest car manufacturer on the planet for the last eighty years, it might be helpful for you. Ask 'why?' and then ask 'why?' of the answer to the why.

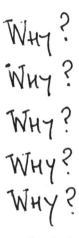

Why is that true? Why do you think that? Why do you believe that's the only possible outcome?

Rather than asking 'What?' first, ask 'Why?' You may well find soul solutions to problems you have been trying to fix with activity for years.

Now ask, 'How?' And 'Who?' Finally ask, 'What?'

THE POWER OF A QUESTION MARK

Great questions are the work tools of curiosity.

As you prepare your meeting agenda, give room for dialogue, where

147 Jeffrey Liker and Gary L. Convis, *The Toyota Way to Learn Leadership: Achieving and Sustaining Excellence through Leadership Development* (McGraw Hill, 2011), p119.

complex issues can be turned over and seen from a variety of angles. Prepare curious questions, then listen for differing perspectives. The stimulating conversations that could ensue will only be provoked by the questions you dare to ask. Resist the urge to settle for simplistic solutions, hurry the dialogue, run to siloed positions, or skip to a conclusion. Just sit in shrapnel of the questioning.

As you write your next visionary keynote, try not to run straight to tight arguments, but ask great questions that spark curiosity. Your audience will find your presentations more compelling and useful.

In performance reviews, know you will encourage deeper development in your colleague if your suggestions are framed as questions designed to encourage reflection, ownership and self-directed growth.

TWO EARS, ONE MOUTH

In your fight to be curious, more than just asking questions, you must also learn to listen deeply to responses. Try all you can to listen to understand, not to make a better point.

Listen to their heart, the feelings they're expressing. Listen to their mind, the thoughts they're attempting to articulate. Listen for their background, the traditions they might be walking in, the experience they will be speaking from, and the culture they carry. Listen to their soul. Not only will you honour them in so doing, but you will learn and grow as you do. And your eventual responses will be better.

Curiosity is, you see, the practice of the teachable. I used to be of the view that anyone can be coached into a better leader. I have since had to revise that opinion and I am now quite comfortable in firing clients who have proved over time that they are not coachable. I'm sure you've met these people, many of whom appear to operate as if they are the sole arbiters of truth, they already know all things they really need to know! These leaders tend to lead in echo chambers, they may seem to be listening, but they are not really hearing, rarely applying, changing or growing.

The curious walk in the opposite spirit. They welcome new thinking, they invite the discomfort of disagreement and they push into intellectual stretches.

My wife, Niki, is a grief and bereavement counsellor and an incredible listener. She will give you full and undivided attention when listening to your story. Even though she has many demands on her time, when she's engaging with you, you are all that matters. It's a natural ability and a skill she works at. Her secrets are curiosity and compassion. Niki is genuinely interested in people, their stories, their challenges and their potential.

There are many techniques she has honed over years of listening well, but what I find most instructive is what she does with her assumptions. Niki marries her assumptions, firstly, to curiosity before she makes any judgments; it creates a path for world class listening and helps her lead with soul. Contrary to populist thinking, assuming is not wrong, or the problem, it just makes you human. Assumptions get you out of bed in the morning, confident that the ground can hold you. They are neutral. It's what you bolt onto an assumption that makes it constructive or destructive.

Assumption + Judgement = CLOSED

Assumption + Curiosity = OPEN

AND, BUT AND OR

It's not only assumptions that can become roadblocks to curiosity; the words you use to punctuate your conversations also have power to restrict you. Have you realized how often you use the word 'but' to continue a conversation? And if you have, have you also considered how that word disables learning, growth and even relationships? Equally, have you considered how 'or' might be shutting down your thinking and possibilities?

No? I hadn't either until a friend pointed it out. I thought I was pretty open minded, yet I was inadvertently restricting options and alternatives, undermining creativity, becoming predictable and mediocre.

So, I'm trying to teach myself to stop saying 'but' and 'or'! It's surprisingly difficult. Try 'AND' I was told. The suggestion annoyed me. And then, freed me.

If you can learn to lead with 'Yes, and … ', it's a launch pad for curiosity, creativity and inclusivity.

WHO GETS YOUR EARS

All conversations are not equal; all listening is not either!

The leader who would lead from their soul must choose well what they listen to, who they converse with and how they engage, turn their ear to wise counsel and turn it away from simplistic opinion. Any cursory scroll of social media will make my point for me, it's a 'hot mess'! Opinion and puerile thought blended with incisive comment and meaningful content, a waste of time and a well of wisdom.

Choose for wisdom and experience, choose for curiosity, for a wondering leader, sometimes even choose for age!

What you do in your virtual listening, do even more so in your actual listening. Who are your counsellors? Take every opportunity to sit at the feet of someone you admire, who has walked longer, thought deeper and led better than you, it's going to be invaluable. Get curious about their wounds, their scars, their priorities and patterns and allow their counsel to satisfy your current questioning and fill your future with greater wisdom and wonder.

Your curiosity plus their experience will grow your leadership. And then, when it really matters, apply that learning to landing an airliner full of passengers on a river. In fact, what really matters is applying that curious learning to the curious learning of others.

A CULTURE OF CURIOSITY

'Our education system doesn't educate, it qualifies. Our interest has become knowledge when it should be wisdom.'

A number of years ago, I found myself talking about learning with a friend who is an experienced educator. He was young enough to not care if he were caught in a cynical opinion and just senior enough to get away with it even if he was.

He had interesting thoughts on a return to Socratic methods, a bias towards creative thinking and an insistence of the study of human interaction and relationships. The core of his solution, was however, a return to apprenticeship and mentoring as foundational to education.

'Humans learn best through apprenticeship,' he postured, and I agree. We are wired to learn most when we 'go and see', 'ask why', 'marginally improve', and 'never arrive'. We learn because we have seen, imitated and applied, not because we have been told. The latter develops followers, the former, leaders.

The pursuit of the curious flourishes in and perpetuates a culture of apprenticeship. Organizations in which each employee has a map and a guide, a mentor who is invested in their growth and a path for their development. These are businesses whose daily activity is done in partnership, mentors passing on technical skills, encouraging leadership performance from a deep well of real-life experience, and encouraging and responding to curious questions. In our coaching model, we use the following tool to encourage this practice:[148]

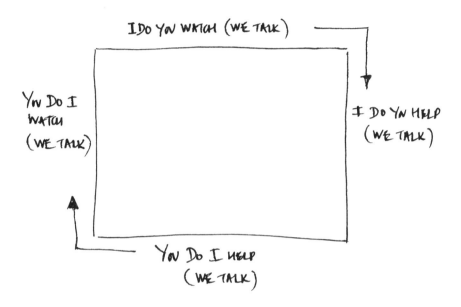

I call the model I borrowed and doctored the Apprenticeship Square. It's a journey around the square that's going to take a proclivity towards curiosity from both the mentor and the apprentice to make the trip.

I'll bet a gut reaction as you read it is that your leadership life is too busy for this. But this is the vital work of your leadership life. So, you can't afford not to do this; reading on is largely about figuring that out.

---

148 I tried to find out who authored this model, but it has been iterated on by many. An early apprenticeship model was provided by David Ausubel in his book *Educational Psychology: A Cognitive View* (1968) and the model was developed further by Allan Collins, John Seely Brown, and Ann Holum in their book *Cognitive Apprenticeship: Making Thinking Visible* (1989). The Cognitive Apprenticeship Research Laboratory at Northwestern University has progressed this as well. Giant Worldwide uses a version credited to A. Maslow, Gordon Training International.

I do, you watch

Your team, at this stage, is unconsciously incompetent. But you're not! They need you to dial back from your unconscious competencies; to make conscious for you, and then for them, what has become second nature. They need to hear you work out what you do and how you do it. So intentionally pull them in close, invite them into conversations they should observe, have them eat lunch with you while you think through an issue at hand out loud. They need your stories, your perspectives, your voice. Generously give room for their curious questions.

Barnabas Rigden Green is a leading consultant vascular surgeon. He's one of these Soul Leaders. Barney has developed an almost automated apprenticing habit as he operates. In his theatre, whoever is gowned up, whatever their role in the procedure, must listen to a forensic commentary of every specific aspect of the job at hand. From the washing of hands through the surgery itself, he says what he sees in obsessive detail, never assuming they already know something.

I do, you help

Your team is now consciously incompetent – they know they don't know much (and it's freaking them out). But you do! Don't dazzle from a distance, but give them a little room to get their hands dirty alongside you. Open your schedule to them. You don't need to add a huge number of extra meetings, just cheat a little.

If I'm travelling, I may as well travel with someone and give them a role. As I prepare a keynote, I might as well ask for help with a portion. To release a new generation of leaders, you don't have to become busier, but you may need to invite others to help, even where you don't need it.

This is where Barney invites the observers who've become learners to be participants. He says, 'Tell me what you see?' and 'What comes next?' It's as though he asks those in his operating room to coach him.

You do, I help

At this point, the roles have changed. They are in the driver's seat, although you can get a hand on the wheel, if necessary.

This process, if practised properly, is going to irritate you. It slows you down. You'll want to just do it yourself. But younger leaders will need to fail and make a mess on your watch, with your reputation on the line and with your relational and leadership capital exposed and vulnerable. You'll have some messes to clear up. But that's what it takes to lead with soul.

In Barney's operating room, once his students have proven they're ready, the tools are in their hands. His commentary takes new shape: 'Talk me through what you're doing ... ' As the mentor, make room for curious questions.

The length of tether you give will obviously depend on the context (Barney's operating room leaves no space for life-impacting error), but give all the room you can for them to give it a go. How will anyone learn if they don't have a shot?

You do, I watch

This is when the leader becomes a fan. Your team's experience is becoming unconscious competence. You may have no functional leadership role, but you're leading from a distance, there to advise when asked.

You cast a shadow as a leader. Your shadow covers and protects, but it can also *over*shadow. You can intentionally or unintentionally stifle the very confidence and competence that you are trying to release. You must get out of the way. You must learn to be absent well.

Curiosity is a dedication to mastery, and cultivating the pursuit of mastery in others. But it is also a step into mystery, accepting you will not fully know how things will turn out.

This journey around the square, if done well, is clearly developmental for your emerging talent. At the same time it offers possible future solutions for the complex succession planning that most organizations find so challenging. The benefit of the model is not, however, restricted to just these two applications. In leading someone around the square, the curious leader remains curious and retains wisdom and continues to grow in impact.

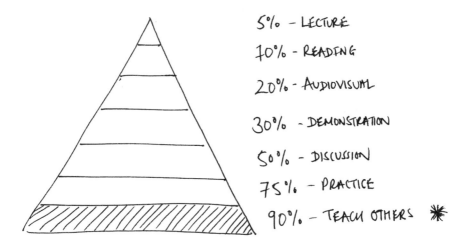

5% – LECTURE

10% – READING

20% – AUDIOVISUAL

30% – DEMONSTRATION

50% – DISCUSSION

75% – PRACTICE

90% – TEACH OTHERS ✳

Just in case you haven't got pyramid fatigue, here is another one. This tool illustrates the protégé effect[149] – the idea that you learn best by teaching the subject matter. 'While we teach, we learn' – or so believed Seneca, the Roman philosopher.[150] The point the model makes for public communication is self-evident – go beyond lecturing if you want people to truly understand. The application for apprenticing is the same. We lose what we don't pass on, and deeply retain that which we do. Apprenticing is, in this way, as redemptive for the leader as it is seminal for the student. If the curious leader does not take this seriously, their learning will atrophy, dissipate and age-out.

149 Jean-Pol Martin, 'The Protégé Effect: When Teaching Others Improves Our Own Learning' in *Educational Psychology Review 1*, no. 4 (1989), pp357–369.
150 Seneca, 'Letter 81' in *Letters to Lucilius*, translated by Robin Campbell (Penguin Books, 1969), pp181–185.

A CURIOSITY BIAS

Another story of the little corporal, Napoleon. I'm not sure this is a true story, but it makes a great point. My father passed it on and I've applied it to great effect in my leadership.[151]

'You get to choose who you lead and who you lose!' he said emphatically to me. I was bemoaning the levels of opposition and churn in the organization I was trying to lead, and he was trying to get me to prioritize apprenticeship. He went on to tell me Napoleon would divide his army into thirds.

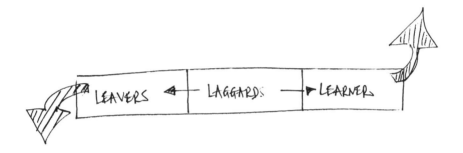

Napoleon (allegedly!) believed a third of his forces were so loyal to him, the empire and the cause, that when they caught sight of the enemy, he had to hold them back from just attacking. They were up for it!

With another third, he had the opposite problem. Made up of conscripts and criminals, they were disloyal, didn't care about the empire, and had no real love for Napoleon. In contrast, when they saw the enemy, they were more likely to desert, to run away.

The final third, Napoleon reasoned were waiting to see who was going to win the argument. Are we attacking or fleeing?

My father explained that in his experience, most leaders

---

151 My father isn't the only one to have passed along this anecdote. It's often attributed to Napoleon and is thought to have persisted through oral tradition, although never recorded as a first-hand account.

deployed almost all their energy trying to persuade the leavers not to leave. Consequently, three things happen.

1. The Learners leave: They want to be invested in, promoted and developed. What they experience is very little attention. They think you're oblivious to their talent, which quenches their enthusiasm. They leave you to find what they need in someone else.

2. The Laggards learn: They learn that if they threaten to leave and act in a disloyal manner, they can get your attention and input. So that's how they act, and over time they create a culture of fear and discontent (with your help).

3. The Leavers leave: You can't stop them. They are not loyal to you or your cause and no amount of your investment is going to change that. They may well do better following another leader with another cause.

You get to choose who you invest your time in. I say: choose for curiosity. Choose those who are up for growing and keen on learning from you and invest your time disproportionately. Choose to give most energy to Learners, give no oxygen to the Leavers, and give grace to the Laggards. Trust that your attention given to the curiosity of the Learners will create a culture of keenness in those whose disposition is to wait and see.

How do you know a Learner so you can invest? Look for the True, the Brave and the Kind – you can train competences and capacities later. But make sure you back a Learner.

COLLECTIVE CURIOSITY

Whether the task at hand is problem solving, creative ideation or culture codification, the importance of establishing a process of curiosity for your team and organization cannot be overstated. You simply cannot innovate in a healthy way without it.

Walt Disney was without doubt one of the most creative minds of the entertainment industry and achieved massive success as a result. It is said, by those who worked alongside him, there were three Walts: Walt the Dreamer, Walt the Realist and Walt the Critic. His legacy endures, in part, in a brilliant design mirroring the personality of the man himself. A creative process was inspired that includes three rooms: an Ideation Room for dreaming, an Editing Room for realism and a Critic's Room to fail any deficient project, and to do so in the room rather than outside of it.[152] The process is particular and exacting but results in repeated brilliance.

Imagine how integrated the process of curiosity might be if you could have these same three rooms in your offices:

Room 1 (Ideation Room): Is only for dreaming – nothing else is allowed. Share the broadest ideas possible, no filtering, no realism and no spoilers allowed.

Room 2 (Editing Room): Is for realism. We reduce possibility according to what we know about the world. If the Ideation Room is 'money is no object and anything is possible,' the Editing Room is 'let's get real about what is truly possible.'

Room 3 (Critic's Room): Is for spoilers (Disney animators called this experience the 'sweatbox'[153]). This room is for putting the project under the microscope. It reduces our ideas to tears and our options to *one*. This room is, importantly, 'us against the idea' not 'us against each other'. In these Critic's meetings, no holds are barred, as it's better to fail in this room than to be exposed in the marketplace.

---

152 This concept it often attributed to Walt Disney, and codified by Robert Dilts' observations of Disney's creative process in his 1995 book, *Strategies of Genius: Volume 1.*
153 Interviews from former animators such as Ward Kimball and Frank Thomas detail the rigor of what they called 'a very tough experience' and 'a place where you could get your ideas killed, but also a place where you could get your ideas made.'

Even if you don't have the luxury of three rooms to give over to this process (or even one), embrace the discipline. Use three pieces of paper, or three different meetings or ask people to put on different hats.

Give your team permission to dream before creating a plan and acting on it. This will likely test your patience and you'll probably feel an impulse to press forward before this process has truly breathed, but if you do, you will find their plans will be better and their actions more effective.

Of course, the implication is that you must have a team full of curiosity. You must either wear your own curiosity in a way that others want in on or have a formalized process of curiosity. Better yet, have both.

A CURIOUS LIFE

If you want wisdom, you must have wonder; if you would grow soulfully, you must risk your comfort; and if you would lead vibrant and creative teams, you must make space for the kind of imaginative inquiry we have spoken of here.

And you must keep wanting it; continue to 'go after' it. There is a reason I named the activity of this quality a 'pursuit'. It's a perpetual hunt, an unending chase. If it is not so in you, all that you have gained in growing True, Brave and Kind will die back a little.

This is, then, not a trivial problem. You have to fight to keep at it, to continually rediscover it, and then to keep it, because without it, you cannot lead with soul.

One of my friends decided to start studying for his pilot's license in his early sixties. Having never flown a plane before, he had to learn about navigation, weather patterns, instrumentation and all kinds of mathematic formulas that he thought he'd left behind at school. Despite being one of the most intelligent people I have ever met, he told me that it was about the hardest thing he had ever undertaken. I asked him why he did it; his first response was that he wanted to keep his brain active, challenged and nubile. It is so vital that you keep your mind fit, thinking nimble and your brain stretched. The fact that flying was so stretching was the point of the exercise; his newfound ability to pilot me up the coast is an added benefit.

You don't need to take up flying, but you might need to shock your brain into a curated curiosity.

Start a book group and insist on reading stretching material. Invite interesting people, who will not agree with you, to a supper club and initiate Kind but provocative conversation. Take up a new sport that requires a level of learning in an activity that is alien to you. Enroll in a college course that piques your interest and go deep into the subject.

Do it. It will train your brain, enlarge your heart and exercise your soul. Set yourself one challenge a week that will stretch you.

And keep exploring the thing you do better than anyone else. I love the discipline and art of leadership, so I read biographies (I'm currently reading one on Martin Luther King), watch documentaries, or 'TED Talks' and, of course, I write about it. Choose carefully what leaders, what authorities to trust and invest your time in. For me these are the Scriptures, from which I draw deeply, and, with wonder and wisdom, seek to grow. For you, it might be something else, but show up Curious to your field, invest intentionally, find new ways to think and fresh ways to lead. More than just a thirst for knowledge, wisdom, in this regard, is a quest to seek out, discern, apply and grow throughout a life.

CURIOSITY LEAKS

When you meet the opposite of curiosity, it might present as arrogance or ignorance, and yet, it is more likely the result of passive and resigned acceptance. It shows itself in an inability to learn, pivot and grow. You can't reframe, refresh or reboot. The opposite of curious is soulless. So, fight for this. Fight for:

Go and see
Ask 'Why?'
Marginally improve.
Never arrive.

Sit on your 'buts' and 'ors' and offer 'and' instead. Dream, edit and criticize. Apprentice, apprentice, apprentice and above all, never stop learning ... even after 20,000 hours.

THE CAVE

'The quest of the True'
At the start of the day set yourself for the day. Be real.

THE ROAD

'The way of the Brave'
In the midst of the day keep your eyes on the prize. Be purposeful.

THE TABLE

'The art of the Kind'
At a moment in the day gather your people. Be connected.

THE FIRE

'The pursuit of the Curious'
At the close of the day process your day. Be teachable.

CHAPTER 11

ORDERED

Our goals can only be reached through the vehicle of a plan, in which we must fervently believe, and upon we must vigorously act. There is no other route to success.[154]

PABLO PICASSO

He, who every morning plans the transactions of the day, and follows that plan, carries a thread that will guide him through a labyrinth of the most busy life.[155]

VICTOR HUGO

The mind that opens to a new idea, never returns to its original size.[156]

ALBERT EINSTEIN

CURIOUS AND COMFORTABLE ARE NOT COMPATIBLE

You get what you plan to get.

Company A gets this Soul Leadership deal. This business doesn't just use people to make profit – it respects people, develops them ... and makes profit. It offers some flexibility as far as space and time, and real understanding about the life events that are part of all of our experience: sickness, kids at home, appointments, etc. It has a

154 M.D. Sharma, *Top Inspiring Thoughts of Pablo Picasso: M.D. Sharma's Collection of Artistic Wisdom and Creativity* (Prabhat Prakashan, 2021).
155 Unknown Author, *Popular Educator* (Educational Publishing Company, 1903), p178.
156 Albert Einstein, Alice Calaprice ed., *The Ultimate Quotable Einstein* (Princeton University Press, 2013), p222.

mental health app available to all their employees and a retainer with a coaching business that is used by most. This business has incredibly creative and bespoke onboarding for new hires and thought-through celebration events and compensation packages. Company A has a clear values statement and a compelling vision that is universally understood and simple, relevant systems for feedback and execution. Not surprisingly, its approval rating among workers and clients is continually 'through the roof' and its retention rate is 'best in class.'

It's a set up. It's HIHO.

Company B is different. It believes business is business, life is life, and a careful curation of culture is in direct opposition to the bottom line. In Company B, there is little flexibility, the office hours are set, time off is policed, processes lack malleability and extenuating life events are deemed irrelevant. People are treated more as fuel for the system or parts of the machine. The reward is the job itself and the pay packet. Company B does onboard, but it's 'hit and miss', depending on who is overseeing it. Not surprisingly, the churn in the organization is high, the commitment to roles is minimal and the long-term profitability of Company B is being significantly compromised.

You get what you plan to get. Or don't plan.

Personally, I hate the hard sell of a service plan, the kind that that seems to come necessarily attached to a purchase of anything technical, mechanical or electrical (dishwasher, dryer, blender, speaker, drill). I never buy the plan. I suspect it will come back to bite me at some point, but it hasn't yet.

However, when it comes to the car I own and the house I live in, I have a service plan, several insurances and a maintenance schedule. If something is worth enough to me to want to keep it for a long time, I'll make routine investments to keep it working. If it's vital for your house and your car, it's more so for your soul. And the souls of those you lead.

Get a plan. Stick to the plan. But make sure you enact the plan. And renew it. Make sure you refresh it, use it, mend it, keep at it. Or it will become the thing you once did, the person you used to want to be. The rhythm you kept and that kept you. The leader you thought you might become, but never did.

The second law of thermodynamics[157] applies here: entropy happens to everything. People age, they get wrinkles, backache and reading glasses. Creation itself erodes, icecaps melt, coastlines crumble. Your domestic appliances are just not made to last, and your microwave will fail just after the warranty period runs out. Everything moves towards breaking down, breaking up or just breaking. More virulently if you don't intervene, service it, mend it, clean it or care for it.

It should come, then, as no surprise that left unattended, your leadership also breaks down. Your purpose, goals and agreements fade and fail. If you don't attend to your agreements, you will find yourself in disagreement with them. If you don't pay attention to your cadence, the way you walk through your leadership world will likely become dis-cadent.

As you have possessions you must care for, with a maintenance plan, you also have entrustments you must steward, with a soul plan.

ENTRUSTMENTS & INVESTMENTS

Every human being is born into this world endowed with agency in at least five ways. 3DM International refers to this agency as 'capital'.

---

157 Joseph Kestin, *The Second Law of Thermodynamics* (Dowden, Hutchinson & Ross, 1976).

The five capitals: Financial, Intellectual, Physical, Relational, Spiritual.

Here's how I refer to them and list them in hierarchy, five entrustments carried in greater or lesser quantities by all:

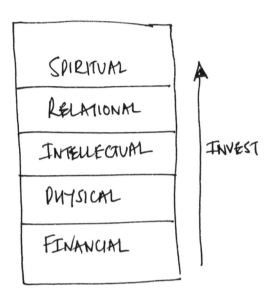

We invest in these things through how we spend our time and resources. For the most part, the leadership cultures we operate in seem obsessed with the lower three of these endowments: financial, intellectual and physical. And we're often neglectful of the top two: relational and spiritual.

While it would be unhelpful to suggest that your soul resides only in the top endowment, it would be unfair to suggest that Soul Leaders are not concerned to grow in all five – they are. It's just that they are investing upwards. A disproportionate amount of time, attention and resources must be given to the top two for a deeper and longer lasting return.

Every leader has entrustments, so every leader must make investments. Take what you've been given, invest it for a return (Truly, Bravely, Kindly, Curiously).

It's not that you have control over everything that happens to you, not at all – although you probably have more influence than you allow yourself to believe. But it is true that how it will go for you is largely dependent on how you plan it will go for you.

You get what you decide to get.

If you decide to make space for your soul, make plans for your days, pursue dreams for your life, invest your entrustments, you stand a chance of being the leader you desire to be. If you don't, you won't!

Your soul will not remain healthy if it is unattended.

SOUL SPACE

I guess the thoughts that follow walk in the opposite spirit of much of the leadership advice I used to be fueled on:

Live life to the max
Lead full and die spent
Suck the marrow out of it all

I know why I bought it. It sounds passionate, adventurous, pioneering and bold. What I discovered, to my cost, is that these sound-bite platitudes caused precisely the opposite outcome that they purport to inspire. Max comes the opposite way.

And yet the temptation is to live life with little margin, to lead tired and on the brink of burnout, and to be dreadful at modeling leadership health to anyone else.

I've counselled and coached many leaders caught in a leadership hamster wheel. They can't stop, but they are breaking. Or won't stop because they are broken. But they will end up with no choice but to stop. Stop will happen to them. If you don't create margin, margin may well be all you have.

In an era of remote working, virtual teams and digital nomads, there is a strong likelihood of there being no boundaries around a working day, a working week or a working year. Unless these things are artificially introduced by you – like breakwaters or groynes on a beach – you will not have a cadence that includes a stop, a pause or a slow. You cannot lead well from that space or at that pace.

Making space for your soul is the only way I know to help you stop. Every retreat sets up the hope of the next leadership season. And every weekend sets up the potential of the next week. And every evening sets up the possibility of the next day. You get what you plan to get.

WHAT TO CONSIDER BEFORE YOU PLAN

Three connected practices help me lay the foundation for my maintenance pattern. Don't get practical until after you've been purposeful.

1. Begin at the end: You must articulate who you are and how you act when at your best. If you don't, how will you know what to aim at and how will you know if you have hit the target?

Can you see it in your mind's eye? Can you see your future leadership self?

What does True look like for you?
What does the most authentic version of you do?
How are you experienced?

What does Brave look like for you?
What are you pursuing?
How are you impacting?

What does Kind look like for you?
How are you connecting?
What is the nature of the team you are building?

What does Curious look like for you?
How are you growing?
What are you learning?
Who is growing alongside you?

2. Perform a pre-mortem on your future leadership self: Assume failure or even death of the project. What did your leadership self die of? How did it come about? What did you neglect, ignore, hold onto, continue, forget, ingest … that killed your soul? Let's fail this now, in theory, so we can succeed later, in reality.

3. Ask for honest and detailed feedback: What does it look like to be on the other side of me?
Where am I stuck in same old thinking?
Where am I surrounded with echo chamber counsellors?
Where could I shake it up?

If you don't do 360 reviews, start now. Institute your own and ask some truthful people awkward questions. Have a number of people hold a mirror up to your leadership and ask these questions:

What difficult conversations do I naturally avoid?
Which attitudes or responses get me stuck or limit my progress?
What do you wish I would just stop doing?
What do you wish I would start doing?

You must have all three:
An idea of what success looks like.
Clarity around what could cause its failure.
An outside view that is honest and kind.

Before we get tactical, let's stick with the big picture.

RETREAT IS TO ADVANCE

Drones have changed the world as we see it. High school video projects and low budget small business promotional films will never be the same again.

They might be controversial and increasingly restricted, but they offer us an ability to see our world and our lives from a perspective that otherwise we wouldn't.

A drone's eye view.

You need one on your leadership. A bigger picture. A longer view. A fresh perspective. Retreat offers just this.

Sometimes you don't know how much you've changed, how far you've come, whether you're still on track, or stuck in a rut. Retreat is time out to reset in order to advance.

Take a day (more if you can) and curate for yourself a wide-ranging and honest review. Lay your agreements out before you.

TRUE – Review your identity.
BRAVE – Review your purpose.
KIND – Review your team environment.
CURIOUS – Review your growth.

What is the real state of those agreements?

Where am I stuck or stale or sick?

How I am applying these agreements in the arena of my entrustments?

SPIRITUAL
RELATIONAL
PHYSICAL
INTELLECTUAL
FINANCIAL

It might help to use a simple tool I offer to my clients.[158]

What is right?
What is wrong?
What am I missing?
What is confused?

Is there a Truer, Braver, Kinder, more Curious leader still to be found? Are there better investments to be made?

Now ask yourself the activity questions:
What will I do now?
What are my 'must win' battles for this new season?

CRAFT YOUR MAINTENANCE PLAN

A philosophy isn't a plan. A plan shows up on your calendar, not just daily and weekly, but also seasonally and annually.

So, take a critical eye to how you spend your time; carefully curate what will make you or break you. Looking at your current activities to consider which among them are *replenishing* in your

158 This is often called the 4 Helpful Lists, created by Tom Paterson, who architected 'StratOp,' a 3-day strategic planning process, carried forward by the Paterson Center.

leadership work and which *rob* from the future self you're on your way to becoming. More than likely, you'll need to add something replenishing that doesn't yet show up on your schedule. More than likely, what robs you is something not obvious; think hard. Don't let yourself off the hook.

Write them here – and then in your calendar, both additions and subtractions.

ANNUALLY:
Think of the broad scope reset that will set your trajectory.
- Replenishes:

- Robs:

SEASONALLY:
Think of renewal, the activities that help you stay on track, perhaps through a few days off track.
- Replenishes:

- Robs:

WEEKLY:

Think of what sustains you through your unique seven-day rhythm, so you can show up in all your places of responsibility as your best self.

- Replenishes:

- Robs:

DAILY:

This is the Cave, the Road, the Table and the Fire. How might you best position yourself to enter these spaces with soul?

- Replenishes:

- Robs:

Make a plan, review the plan, make space for the plan. Tell others you're close to about the plan so they can support it and understand it. Set yourself up for sustained health. Make it hard for yourself not to do what you most want to do.

WEEKEND IS THE REST

This can and should be a time to restore.

Many of my clients are full on, fast paced, 'go at life' people. They work hard and play hard. They vision, plan, relate and execute with intensity. Working hard is rarely a problem for them, but playing hard might be. It is often sabotaging their needed rest. While it is true that those who work with their heads, might find rest by being active with their bodies (if you write for a living, you could run as a recreation), those who work with their bodies, might do well to consider resting with their minds (if you build in your day job, you might read as you relax). It is truer that if you don't really rest, you will not be restored, and that will lessen your positive impact in just about every area of your life.

The recreational activity you are drawn to and choose is less relevant than the pace at which you do it and the energy you put into it. The danger is that learned behaviours in one arena of life easily bleed over into all.

If your work life involves fitting as many meetings in as you can, running from one to the other, you cannot also do something similar on the weekend, or whenever you get a day off. If your job description and your desire to get ahead gives you too much responsibility, too many tasks to juggle and too few pauses to reflect, if your recreation is to be restoration, it can't just mirror that which patently isn't.

If every day is going to be a school day, some days must be rest days. If I am going to lead with laser-like purpose – bravely – some days need to feel purposeless and slow and some activities need to be thoughtless. Ask yourself, 'What activity do you engage in that puts your brain into auto mode?' Doing this will result in two things:

1. Rest for your thinking
2. Better ideas; your brain in auto-mode is given space to piece information together and align thinking, that's why

you often have your best thoughts in the shower or your eureka moments on a long run.

Not practising this will, more than likely, ensure that you become a one-paced, one-dimensional burnout victim.

So where you normally plan three activities on a Saturday, try one. Where you allow four hours for the round of golf and a quick drink, try five hours and lunch. Where you invite the whole street over for a BBQ with late night dancing as a possibility, try a glass of wine and pizza for two by candlelight.

Slow down. Do less. Now. So that you can speed up and inspire better, later.

EVENING IS THE START

It is interesting to me that my ancestorial heritage (Celtic and Jewish) share a common philosophical belief that the start of the day is the end of the day, not the beginning – the day begins at sundown and not sun-up.[159] Both traditions embrace a sense of pace that has been lost in much of our current cultural context: work from rest, don't rest from work. That's the way we're designed.

Work is noble and purposeful and human and, as such, we owe it to ourselves and to our soul to show up rested, able to give of our best.

Try an experiment. Exchange the hours of 10–12 pm for 6–8 am. Before you close the book in disgust, know this: not much healthy, wholesome and productive happens in those evening hours.

I've discovered that in those night hours, I am terribly unproductive, not even resting well. It is the only time in the day when I might drink alone. When I do, it becomes the most vulnerable time of the day for me to eat what is bad for me. And then I don't sleep as well as I need.

159 The Jewish day begins at sunset and lasts until the next sunset, according to the Torah. Celtic cultures often divided days in half – the light half and dark half, the latter beginning the day.

It sounds sad as I read it back. It isn't that bad. But it's not that good, as a set up for soul. If you don't plan, you won't have a plan. If you don't take a break, you will likely break. Have a go. Do it for a month. See how it feels.

I'm sold on this but I have one caveat: make sure you break the rule, quite often actually. This pattern is helpful until it becomes restrictive.

An intentional late night, just you and the sport, your favourite tipple and snacks, is just brilliant when it's occasional. At the same time, don't let your soul set-up experiment get in the way of your connections and the wonderful conversations that can only happen by firelight, lamp light and candlelight. Just make these the exceptions that prove the rule of working from rest as the best way to lead from your soul.

BIG CHANGES ALWAYS START IN SMALL WAYS

All organizational growth comes from organizational health (not the other way around, as so many want to believe). All organizational health comes from individual health.

Company A became what it is through its leaders. Individually, they have internalized and enacted their own HIHO system that changes how they show up. They are the project, and the impact of their personal work is felt well beyond the circle they stand in. It's contagious. It's directive. It freeing for those around them. It's soulful. It guides decision after decision all the way to a HIHO that is both habituated and systematized.

Company B became what it is through its leaders, too. Full stop.

Many leaders have an altruistic desire to provide a healthy culture for their organizations, and think they can make themselves the exception due to the weight of their position. This is a fallacy that will erode, both for you and all those who depend on you to lead with integrity. If you have no maintenance plan, you will not last – and neither will your company.

So, step back, take a breather, get restored, invest upwards, rest well. It will reset and preserve your soul.

CHAPTER 12

WHAT'S SPOKEN AT THE CLOSE

Every man dies. Not every man truly lives.[160]

WILLIAM WALLACE PLAYED BY MEL GIBSON IN THE
FILM *BRAVEHEART*

What you leave behind is not what is engraved in stone monuments,
but what is woven into the lives of others.[161]

PERICLES

'How long until you retire?'
'What will you do when you start drawing your pension?'
'Where do you want to live in retirement?'
'Do you have a succession plan?'

I'm just not sure what I think about the life stage we call
'retirement'. There is a nagging sense within me that the culmination
of all my life's experience, the successes, failures, learnings and
wisdoms must amount to more than greater golf practice, unlimited
vacation time and a capitulation to becoming overweight and
underfit.

Could it even be that the intellectual capital gained and the life
experience processed means that, health allowing, I am at my most
useful to the society I'm part of in my sixties, seventies and eighties?

I am, of course, aware that the argument in my head grows
louder as I approach these ages. I don't think I have ever been more
aware of how vital and how temporary our time is. How bright our
star can burn and how swiftly it can burn out.

160 William Wallace, *Braveheart* directed by Mel Gibson (Icon Productions, 1995).
161 Most often attributed to Pericles, without authoritative citation.

For all of us, there is a moment when we are a leading part in the in the movie of our life. Known. Needed. Valued. Then, sometimes swiftly, certainly quicker than imagined, whatever your status or role, whether you are well known or not, that moment is gone.

You become yesterday's leader.

You have a moment. Then then that moment is passed.

Don't rush over this just because it's uncomfortable, seems a little negative, perhaps even excessively morbid. I want to provoke you to take hold of your opportunity before it is not your moment anymore.

Pause again here.

I want to close by reminding you of your potential and your mortality.

I have had the unenviable task of burying both of my wonderful parents. As hosts and leaders, they filled rooms, inspired others and loved well. Each died relatively young and abruptly – my father of pancreatic cancer; complaining of a bad back and a sore stomach, he walked into the hospital to be checked over and died in the ward eight days later. He had a wonderfully True, Brave, Kind and often Curious life. He had his faults, as we all do, but he tried to lead from a deeper place, from his soul.

Just over a decade later, I received a call from the UK while working in the US, telling me my mother was declining rapidly and might only have days to live. I made urgent calls, changed my plans, bagged some flights, and then broke every speed limit to get to her. We missed her by ten minutes. I did get to say a choked-up goodbye on speaker phone at around 100 miles an hour on the A19 in northeast England.

My parents tried to lead from their soul – not perfectly, for sure, but I'm left with gratitude for their affection and example, and a desire to carry their principles on in my leadership journey.

I am truly aware that there will be a moment when the face on the front of the memorial 'order of service' will be mine. One day I, like you, will have finished my race, and others, who are still running theirs, will gather.

To be honest, I really hope the church is packed with friends and family and beyond, with those I have impacted and influenced. I don't think this is narcissistic (well, maybe just a little); rather, I think it is the hope of the overflow of intention, purpose and investment. As the service closes and the congregation gathers to eat the cold buffet – with miniature quiches and sausages on sticks, that inevitably follows such events – I trust that the life led and the conversations provoked might inspire others to lead from soul.

With that outcome in view, I ask myself:

Did I fix the character of my times?
Or fritter my gift away?
Did I love people well or prioritize things that, in the last analysis,
are patently less important?
Did I pass on soul or just self?

As I allow those morbid thoughts to sit with me, I become increasingly awake to the excessive amount of energy and focus that is given to having, keeping, maintaining, and preserving stuff that is material, temporary, and, in the above regard, pretty meaningless.

Cars, houses, and luxury goods, researched, coveted, sacrificed for. Broken, mended, left behind.

Left behind.

Its staggering what gets left behind – an engulfing thought as I cleared my parents' house and divided the flotsam and jetsam of two whole lives into piles.

The stuff you want to keep because its valuable.
The items you need to keep because they are meaningful.
The things you throw away immediately.
The possessions you'll give away to charity.
And the collections you'll put in boxes and store in your garage and get rid of eventually.

More than what's left behind, it's staggering to consider how much it must have cost, in purchase and maintenance and time and emotion. And how empty it feels now.

There are other things, equally left behind, with greater import, stronger impact and longer lasting effect. These are the immaterial things.

The inspiration imbibed.
The ethos, philosophy and attitudes adopted.
The wisdom appropriated.
The values inherited and stewarded for others.
The love received and passed on.

Much has been written and is still to be discovered about the latent capacity of human beings, particularly in an age of rapid technological advance and the spectre of Artificial Intelligence. Whatever the vast opportunities and real dangers, I vote we begin with the incomparable and untapped potential of the essence we might call soul.

Do the work.

Be who you might be.

Leave all you can of value.

Endowments.

Investments.

Etchings.

That's what I want to leave.

So, I'm doing the work, and showing up at my life. With Truth and Bravery, with Kindness and Curiosity.

There will come a day when 'the project' for you will appear complete. When you can do no more. Not because you've achieved it all, or there are no more mountains to climb or opportunities to embrace, but rather because you are no more.

There is coming a moment, at least as far as your time on this earth is concerned, when there are no more opportunities to be True, Brave, Kind or Curious.

No more mornings in the Cave or interruptions on the Road. No more Tables to sit at or Fires to reflect around. Your time will be done.

You have a choice as to whether you host a pre-mortem, whether you work out what could fail in your imagination, so that you can correct it in reality, present and responsible for it.

But you can be sure there will be a post-mortem you will not be there for. What will be said? By your soul companions and your close friends, by your work colleagues and your grandchildren?

How will you be described? And what will have been passed on, stewarded by you, bequeathed to those who follow you?

The memory of you will fade. You know that's true. Your memory of those you've loved and lost is less than it was, and one day will be faint, and then gone.

But that which has been sown into those who were impacted by you, that which was spoken and imbibed and patterned and repeated, will be internalized and maybe even eternalized.

An etching of the soul.

An etching of the soul leaves a lasting impression.

As miserable as it seems to end a book here, here we must end it. For at the close you have no choice – no more opportunity to write your legacy. It has been written.

But now, you still do have choice. A choice to:

Begin in the Cave
Navigate the Road
Discuss around the Table
And process by the Fire

21 grams is not a lot of weight, but it is the weightiest part of you.